BOA
EDITIONS LTD

YOUR
EMERGENCY
CONTACT
HAS
EXPERIENCED
AN
EMERGENCY

YOUR EMERGENCY CONTACT HAS EXPERIENCED AN EMERGENCY

CHEN CHEN

AMERICAN POETS CONTINUUM SERIES NO.194

BOA Editions, Ltd. ◆ Rochester, NY ◆ 2022

First Edition
22 23 24 25 7 6 5 4 3 2 1

For information about permission to reuse any material from this book, please contact The Permissions
Company at www.permissionscompany.com or email permdude@gmail.com.

Publications by BOA Editions, Ltd.—a not-for-profit corporation under section 501 (c) (3) of the United States
Internal Revenue Code—are made possible with funds from a variety of sources, including public funds from
the Literature Program of the National Endowment for the Arts; the New York State Council on the Arts, a state
agency; and the County of Monroe, NY. Private funding sources include the Max and Marian Farash Charitable
Foundation; the Mary S. Mulligan Charitable Trust; the Rochester Area Community Foundation; the Ames-
Amzalak Memorial Trust in memory of Henry Ames, Semon Amzalak, and Dan Amzalak; the LGBT Fund of
Greater Rochester; and contributions from many individuals nationwide. See Colophon on page 158
for special individual acknowledgments.

Cover Design: Sandy Knight
Cover Art: *Moonlight Photosynthesis* by Vincent Chong
Interior Design and Composition: Michelle Dashevsky
BOA Logo: Mirko

BOA Editions books are available electronically through BookShare, an online distributor offering Large-
Print, Braille, Multimedia Audio Book, and Dyslexic formats, as well as through e-readers that feature text
to speech capabilities.

Cataloging-in-Publication Data is available from the Library of Congress

BOA Editions, Ltd.
250 North Goodman Street, Suite 306
Rochester, NY 14607
www.boaeditions.org
A. Poulin, Jr., Founder (1938-1996)

JUL 1 9 2023

Life is a sack—with holes—and you carry it, you carry it.

— *Marina Tsvetaeva, tr. Ilya Kaminsky*

Lick my butt
cos I'm an angry ethnic fag
& I'm in so much pain
so lick my butt

— *Justin Chin*

for J.
& G.

Contents

III

IV

◆

A Favorite Room

Down the sideways face, through the dilapidated waterfall,
we entered late afternoon's house
& a favorite room: the room of the butterfly skeleton.

Intricate, delicate, somehow not an ounce of tragic.
So beautiful we thought we could have perfect
unswollen gums, be less predictable
gay men, obsessed with our mothers.

It whispered: the new year will bring more coffee flavors,
& sodas, overall more beverage-related upheavals.

It advised us never to buy anything
fresh again, & thus we could be just like it—

Never misspelling a state capital.
Never missing a coworker's birthday.
Always just pretending to be dead.

Summer

after Sarah Gambito

I have a canoe that gives me therapy my insurance won't cover.

The man I love calls from Colorado, unaware of my canoe.

It offers a better kind of cognitive behavioral, in very turquoise water.

The man says his mother is dying & I say *I know* but nothing is clear.

I pay the canoe with my best Christopher Walken impressions.

It becomes clear that Colorado is where all calls are from, how did I not know.

He says his mother has a couple of months.

The canoe says to eat five cookies, then canoe off the calories.

He says he saw snow in New Mexico on the way to Colorado.

I see how my past is a nun who knows a lot of state birds & my future is a pancake-
   shaped abyss.

He says his sister is having a child.

He says it's snowing & his sister is pregnant & his mother is dying so they
   probably won't be able to go on as many rides at Disney.

I say *okay* & *I see* but neither is true.

The sky shuts its geese-filled mouth.

Between the canoe & me there is no more discourse.

I wait for him to come back. I wait for Colorado to go away.

Doctor's Note

Please excuse Chen Chen from class. He is currently dead. He came in last Thursday, exhibiting clear signs of dying, such as saying in a clear voice, *I am nothing except the wish to listen to Coldplay*, & after one too many plays of their 2002 hit "The Scientist," he is dead. Though few have improved from this condition, Chen Chen has been prescribed long baths in chicken stock & more recent music. Also, some rudimentary Tai Chi early each morning in his room with the curtains drawn. Medically speaking, Chen Chen's current state is very gross. It would be unwise, however, to try to force Chen Chen, physically or with the promise of new *Buffy* episodes, back into life. It would be unwise & gross to reach out to Chen Chen's parents. They are not his emergency contacts & have exhibited clear signs of wishing he were dead, such as saying in a clear voice, *You'd be better off dead. Better than whatever you are with other men.* Of course, after learning of Chen Chen's death, they fell to their knees, into a state commonly referred to as "utter devastation." & it was, in a medical sense, satisfying to hear of their "utter devastation." But studies show that this state is ultimately bupkis. Studies predict that if Chen Chen recovers, it will take around three months for his parents to find his fully restored state unsatisfying. Or, if he remains his remains, they will find themselves fully content with the memory of Chen Chen, their sweet Chen Chen, before he became so whatever he was. They will think of him, so fondly, while sharing a bowl of strawberry ice cream, the last thing they remember him loving.

Higher Education

I eat bad tomatoes   his mother discontinues treatment
we are in another state   flat   far
I professionally develop   he won't watch the scary movie
we hold hands if we are close   to the University

my friend calls   asks *Is this a bad time*
his mother has a fever   everywhere   my friend calls
says *I can't fix it   anything   I need   help*
I study to become a teacher   a friend   a useful   hand

his mother becomes a fact   we are   flat   far
I learn where the free food is   he learns to say   *She was*
we learn to say *I'm fine* to shout *You don't know   you just don't*
we refuse   to learn leaving   we hold·

& hold   each other's sleep   we dream
& climb   the tallest   leafiest   tree

Summer

You are the ice cream sandwich connoisseur of your generation.

Blessed are your floral shorteralls, your deeply pink fanny pack with travel size
    lint roller just in case.

Level of splendiferous in your outfit: 200.

Types of invisible pain stemming from adolescent disasters in classrooms,
    locker rooms, & quite often, Toyota Camrys: at least 10,000.

You are not a jigglypuff, not yet a wigglytuff.

Reporters & fathers call your generation "the worst."

Which really means "queer kids who could go online & learn that queer
    doesn't have to mean disaster."

Or dead.

Instead, queer means, splendiferously, you.

& you means someone who knows that common flavors for ice cream
    sandwiches in Singapore include red bean, yam, & honeydew.

Your powers are great, are growing.

One day you will create an online personality quiz that also freshens the
    breath.

The next day you will tell your father, *You were wrong to say that I had to change.*

To make me promise I would. To make me promise.

& promise.

The School of Australia

Your emergency contact has called
to quit. Your back-up plan has backed
away. Your boyfriend has joined a boy band
named All Your Former Boyfriends

& Sarah McLachlan. In the ugly
teapot/uglier luggage section of your local
Dillard's, you would like to scream.
Meanwhile, your father has decided

to pursue his original dream & move
to Australia, the brochure version he fell for
in college. In Australia, he will study Beach
Studies & his Western name *Tony*

will finally catch on. *Tony,*
the Australians will say, *where have they been hiding
you?* & Tony will say, *I never imagined I'd be doing
way better than my son.* & on his way home

from the school of the beach, its shells & endless
glitter, Tony will toss out a dog-eared copy
of the manual he received upon arriving in America—
How to Have Deeply Sorrowful Exchanges

with Your Son About Your Immigrant Hardships:
How to Make Him Understand He Must Become
a Neurosurgeon/At Least a Dentist.
The manual will go on to a second career

titling academic papers.
Australia will be renamed Tony's

Son Get Your Shit Together!
TSGYST!

will call to say, *But*
remember? You're already a glittery stretch
of dream. Your own
emergency Tony.

Items May Have Shifted

after & for Muriel Leung
for & after the man on the plane
from Los Angeles to

你的帽子

he says......pointing to

beneath my seat..........I have just........my eyes......stood

up..........I look at him..............at the dropped

color........in a headache.........of landed......light........I look at him

he looks...like my father but younger..my uncle but...haven't seen my family in..

Lubbock........86 degrees......don't forget........你的帽子........he repeats

less sure I understand........but I nod....bend to pick up....my dropped

colorful..............then I want to say......but he's

walking away................through the narrow

bright

because they want to 睡觉

I leave the man's words..........safely

enclosed

in an overhead

because some......many.........do not need them 翻译........because

as I step into the small Lubbock airport

I see my father 睡觉

in a small white room

in Quincy.... 麻州

20

....
....
....................we'd gone to see M. Night Shyamalan's *Signs*.....................
.........I thought it was the best movie ever..
..............................I was fourteen....................my father was...................
....already 睡觉
....
.........I paced around his dark apartment......I moved his one cup for tea...............
........from the kitchen table..............to the kitchen counter............................
....
....the next day I would go.....
..............back to Amherst........my mother.......my brothers........................
....my mother who I'd just seen crying...........
..........................in the too big..
..........................too purple 沙发 she bought at a yard sale.......................
....
....
.......because for so many the words of here live noisy live 隔壁 the words...........
..........................of so-called there..
....
....
.............这个 new job 会帮我们 get our green cards.....I don't remember........
............who said it...........................but it was my father's new job..............
................my father's moving..
....across 麻州..............................
.....................my father's one cup...
....
....
...............because many words are easy enough to look up................................
..........because my father looked...
....unimpressed by the aliens in *Signs*.....yawned at the human family's inability...
.................to stand up.........against...
....
....
........obviously in another story it would have been divorce...not green cards.......
...................or maybe.........in another story....it would have been both..............

....................but they did...我爸妈...fight.....................................
....in the narrow...............................
....color of..
....没睡觉

....

.........because 你滚! 我 headache 我累死了...

....

....

......because still I see the word.....alien.....on neighbor's faces.......because...........
..........as the American story goes...M. Night Shyamalan.....changed his name....
....................in order to make his movies..
....because.....................................
....
......in the bright nowhere...of baggage claim...
.........................waiting among the last......the 累死了...............................
........I am a low-budget production of a man......standing......laughing strange.....
....laughing strange...............

....
....
....
....

....

...............你应该多省钱
            不用来这里看我   my father says
    then
                你要不要去看电影?

The School of Morning & Letters

Assigned to flurries
of dust, assigned to the dead
middle of winter in West Texas,
assigned to give assignments
in a building called English,
I walk to campus, rubbing flecks

of night from my eyes.
On my phone, the morning
headlines spell crisis,
the morning is picture
after picture of the coiffed like
cotton candy doom,

the chalky delirious face
of our leader, endorsed
by the KKK. Assigned
him, assigned this season of k's
& hard c's, I look up & see the dark
birds called grackle,

congregating near English.
I catch, am caught in the winged
weather above food court & student
union. I listen to the grackle
orchestra of unrelenting
shriek. I study the blur

of their long-tailed swerving, their
bodies like comets, frenzied
commas, yet unable, finally,
to mark, to contain
the wide blue Texas sky.
Still, they try. Every beak

& claw, every uncalm feather
tries, as if the sky
were the only fact left,
as if the grackles have been told
to memorize it, as if someone,
someday, will ask them to

speak it, this long blue sentence.

The School of Fury

As Robert Frost said, the best way out is always through.

Or as Alanis Morissette said, the only way out is through.

Or as I said, 8th grade was all Robert Frost & Alanis Morissette.

Because I had to learn who the important white people were.

& we worship immigrant hardship instead of building a house more breathable.

To read & remember & know & say so, without the echo of an accent.

When the white kids knew nothing about Marilyn Chin.

When the white adults know nothing about Lawson Fusao Inada.

When the 30-something white guy in poetry class says *A poem is this*—, based on what a 70-something white guy once said.

& everyone just nods & I want to say *No* & scream & would Frost have called me a chink?

& take everyone through the wound of it.

Through the cat with a hummingbird in its mouth.

Through my much-desired never-fulfilled Halloween costume, which was the wheel from *Wheel of Fortune*.

Through the night my father came to pick me up from a friend's house.

Through the early fall sidewalk. Through Newton, Massachusetts. Outside Boston. Inside whiteness. Through my enjoyment of *The West Wing* with white friends.

Through my father knocking on the wrong door, the neighbor's door. Through the neighbor's door, where you can hear them whispering, deciding to call the police because who is the man at the door, calling in a strange voice?

Through my father almost getting arrested for trying to retrieve his son. Through later, in the car, my father insisting *You gave me the wrong address.* Through *Don't ever give me the wrong address again.* Through my imitations of Frost in 8th grade, which my teacher called *impeccable.* Throughout the town, on every doorstep except ours, a little family of carved pumpkins. Through the happy, happy wounds of their faces. Through *Why don't you try not going to the wrong house next time?* Through hugging my white friends goodbye-yeah-see-you-in-class because nothing was wrong.

Winter

The grackles flap dark & showy into my sleep.

I know they are only my synapses sparking pretty hallucinations but still they flaunt their rough & many consonants.

Kellogg's! Lacuna! Grief counseling!

These are the sounds they like to make.

Then they ask about my mother & father, whether I've spoken to them lately.

In this way, they are just like my boyfriend.

I tell them my cell service is terrible, that I often think of switching, & then the company texts me, *Thank you for being a valued member of our community!*

The grackles say to speak more slowly. They are still learning human.

It starts to snow & I wish I lived alone, in Paris.

Or maybe in my parents' house, without my parents.

My boyfriend's mother lives in a box.

My boyfriend lives with his mother in slow, not quite stories during breakfast.

I wish I wasn't tired of his sadness.

But I'd rather look at the snow, falling like silver confetti, another pretty thing my mind can make.

I wonder if I'd be a better person if I learned to speak bird.

The grackles say I should learn to pick up the phone.

I ask for a different assignment.

Call, the grackles say. *Call back.*

The School of Your Book / Letter to Jennifer S. Cheng

Three nights your book
has held my childhood & nowhood
in its peppermint boat
while a great many flutes were played, probably all

by Björk. Not since my last bowl of chilled,
honeyed lu dou tang have I felt this care, this
so. Welcomed by the brightest,
mooniest *hello.*

Hello, haven't seen you in a
no, don't care, guy
from high school friend's college years. Out
at a housewarming & all I want

is Totoro's Catbus to furball in,
ferry me back,
back to your pages, a fourth night.
How could I have forgotten the beautifully

rude option of just bringing
your book along? Once I brought a book
to a boyfriend's friend's birthday/new job/going
away party. Afterward,

the boyfriend said, *You barely talked*
to anyone. & I said, *Not true.*
You get it. Your book, better than a boyfriend
dipped head to groin to toe in honey,

gets it, has me
unpiling my coat from the coatsiest pile
on the new Ikea daybed
I'm done helping

warm. Your book, with its waiting boat
& sea. Your book, a reminder of how
much more night I could
wade into.

Study Abroad

Hefei, China

Your white classmates treat you like a dictionary with legs
& sometimes you like it.

Some nights, a taxi driver treats you like a local & you love it.
& then you speak

a full sentence. Then he says, *Ah, you're from
Fujian province.* Then you nod because nodding is easier

than saying, *Well actually* & *Massachusetts
& close to Boston & also Amherst & all*

*five Backstreet Boys & originally my father was considering Australia
& the exoskeleton of a wronged lobster & Costco & my mother*

*in Costco considering a lobster & a year
or so in Texas & I was born here but grew up there & I grew up there but*

*was born of soup, both mung bean & primordial
& in the future*

when I'm writing this, I'll be back in Texas, where some will say,
Welcome back, *some,* Go back,

& now it's time to get out of the taxi, begin to walk back
to the dorms.

Walking, you whisper lines from the Dao De Jing,
then from the latest pop song. In lamplight,

you soft-sing to a tall audience
of trees. You're in touch with The Way

as well as The Wants of boys, flaunting such
innovative hair. & the trees give off a silvery

smell that's become your entire
summer. You walk slowly. You want,

you try to ask the smell
what these trees are called.

we'll be gone after these brief messages

god stopped by in his magenta rowboat

i said god you have to stop stopping by
if you're never going to tell me the meaning of life

god said life is meaningless
while language often means too much

my grandmother stopped by & said no
the meaning of life is love
the kind that produces children
why don't you have a girlfriend yet

my mother stopped by & said look
he's busy with his studies stop asking

god got back in his turquoise steamship

life is a joyful thing he said
it's probably very good for you

II

Winter

Big smelly bowel movements this blue January morning.

From the living room TV, a commercial from our TV company: *We're the
fastest, the only—*

Meaning, *Love us above all others.*

What makes poop more pungent on certain days?

A question for science.

From the living room TV: the powerful cite *Law*, bark *Order—*

Meaning, *Love us or else.*

Years ago, a teacher said never to use the word "poop" in a poem.

Today, the icy kiss of the toilet seat wakes me up.

Today, I poop while my boyfriend shouts from the living room, *Did you hear that*,
meaning the atomic scientists who say we are now two & a half minutes
to midnight.

But still I marvel whenever poop comes out as one true Platonic tube.

I am trying to be marvelous.

& to make my enemies throw up.

I mean, if you shower with soap & eat well, maintaining consistent gastrointestinal
health, you should be ready for a rimjob or other forms of anal play.

My boyfriend & I are not platonic.

From the TV: a white supremacist cites *Science*, barks *Two sides to every*—

I mean, up the throat, out the mouth: the fastest, the only way the powerful
     will let go of their shit.

I mean, my boyfriend & I are not into scat but if you are I hope your beloved
     produces the most fragrant, citrusy shit.

I mean, is "shit," is "scat" more or less literary than "poop"?

I mean, one winter night I got sick & pooped the bed.

& he just got up with me.

Helped strip the sheets, carry it all to the washer.

I kept saying, *I'm so sorry*, shivering, *I'm so, I'm sorry*. But he said, *What? Hey.*
     I love you.

The School of Red

The problem with love
lives in a boy's struck
face, a mother's still

raised, ready hand,
a son's *I think I like girls*
& boys ringing in a parent's

heart, a mother's pure
red thumping
yes that knows

better than the head
with its hairy maybes
how to love, without thinking

that maybe she knows
little, maybe nothing
about whether her love

wants this love, needs her
thumping, will survive
her yes, *yes you*

like girls, such pure love
redly addressing
a problem.

a small book of questions: chapter i

this sequence is after Bhanu Kapil

Who are you & whom do you love?

My fingers smell of lime & his sex. My mouth smells of his mouth.

My hair smells of the moment the lawnmower growled by our curtained bedroom window, just as we started touching.

Who are you & whom do you love?

A memory, this memory: my mother saying, *So you're not a boy... & not a girl?* I am fourteen & have just told her maybe I'm not gay, maybe I'm bisexual. She seems even more alarmed. I thought she would be sort of pleased. Her son's not a complete failure! He might still end up with a girl! Marriage! Children! (Grandchildren!) But it seems that fully gay equals more girl than boy. Fully straight equals fully boy, full of happiness. Bisexual equals girl boy boy girl girly boy boyish girl neither both both nobody never anybody too many bodies he's confused. Of course, if I'm gay, I'm also confused. But this bisexuality is a far worse confusion. Chaos. My mother looks at me like I might sprout a set of octopus arms, or like I might shed my body altogether, become a touchless drift, a gust of ghost.

What is the shape of your body?

Two snails: small, very small, exposed, after a rainstorm, on the front steps of a house in West Texas.

What do you remember about the earth?

The truck window rolls down, the man's head comes through, he says, *I'm so sorry, man, I'm sorry, I didn't see you, man,* & his voice grows louder, as though trying to make it all up to me with the volume of his voice. & I say, *It's okay, it's okay,* & even chuckle a little, as though comforting him, the truck, the street, the darkness, the dark. & the whole time I keep wondering: Did he say "man" or "ma'am"? Am I hearing "ma'am" because of that afternoon in Worcester when the bus driver called me "ma'am"? Or that morning at Starbucks: *Excuse me, ma'am?* Or that evening—I call it "that evening" now—in West Texas, the time I was almost hit by a very large, very red truck, & spent most of the moment afterward wondering, "Man" or "Ma'am"?

How will you / have you prepare(d) for your death?

I walk home calmly.

I kiss him.

> I kiss him.
> I forget to tell him about the truck.

Or: I don't tell him because he's told me how often he thinks about death, his & mine, & I don't want to scare him, don't want him thinking & thinking about what could've happened that night, what could happen tonight. How do you tell someone you love them without making them think about one day losing you?

> I kiss him.
> In the moment, I don't think about why I'm not telling him.

How will you live now?

My mother texts me, calls me, leaves me voicemails, emails me, calls. English. Chinese. In the voicemail, she directs me to her email. *Please take a look.* Subject line: *help.* I click. I open. I feel briefly bad that my phone's been on silent all day. Guilty that I haven't been checking. But I feel glad, at the same time, that I didn't have to go through an entire conversation just so I could get to the email & start correcting. My mother has asked me to *please take a look at the following,* to *please correct any mistakes,* & *please do it soon because it is due on November 1,* & it is October 30. She is a high school Mandarin Chinese teacher. In the email, her objectives for the 2016–2018 school years. How she plans on achieving these objectives. During which term. The kind of exercises, quizzes. *Closed book.* I add a hyphen. *Closed-book.* She plans to *put additional resources in class web site.* I correct her: *putting additional resources on the class website.* I highlight my corrections in yellow. I go through four pages of her writing, her inhabiting this bureaucratic language. I'm bored & then impressed. Her writing in English has always been good, but this document is fairly polished & also wordy in that sleep-inducing way I'm sure her department will like. After an hour & a half of alternating between focus & yawns, I send my completed corrections to her. She writes back: *Thanks for your help! I am always not sure when to use "the" or "on."*

Who was responsible for the suffering of your mother?

When I tell my boyfriend the story about helping my mother with her writing, I explain, *In Chinese, there are no definite articles, no "the."* I'm not sure if there is an explanation for my mother's misuse or lack of "on." Sometimes I have no idea which is better to use: "on" or "in." Place your hope *on.* Place your hope *in.* When I search online, most of the sites that appear in the results have to do with passages from the Bible. Place your hope *in* God. *On* God. Though I don't believe in him, it seems rude to place anything *on* God, even hope. I imagine God,

> sitting in heaven, weighed down by all the weighty abstractions people continue to place on him. Hope, immortality, truth, goodness, forgiveness, perfect love. Perfect speech.

What are the consequences of silence?

Another memory, another conversation, the same conversation. *Are you afraid of women because of me?*

I shake my head. I am shaking my head hard (I remember that feeling, shaking my head instead of screaming, though I also did that). I am shaking my head & trying to say calmly, at a normal volume, *I'm not afraid of women. I just don't feel for women what I feel for guys, I guess.*

I want to answer my mother: *No, I'm afraid of you because of you.*

The School of More School

God is a honey
flavored extra strength cough drop.
I am another attempt to confess

I have not read *Ulysses*.
God is a webinar
on how to be closer

to your CV.
I wear faux leather
but engage in some real

kinks. I talk to my neighbors'
cat. I carry 2 pencils & 1 purple pen
at all times. I can't decide

whether the university
is a refuge for the bookish lonely
or a T-shirt store

run by a soda company.
Late at night I go out
to check my mailbox

as though a present
has just been delivered.
Tonight, a handsome bundle

of air. Tonight, I am
not my mucus.
God is how difficult it is

to stay calm.

& then a student stands up, says, *Are you serious?*

       to the student who's still standing,
who's just finished presenting what sounded like
       a Sahara-dry book report—until
the last sentence, *Guns are not the problem,*
       which she said like
an eager teacher, like she was, is, in fact, at the front
       of the classroom.
& then, the classmate. Her *Are you serious?* with a great
       snort of a laugh
that means, *I am serious, I am*
       standing. & I stand up,
from a chair in the back. & everyone goes silent,
       even the student who taps, always
taps his foot against his backpack on the floor, he stops,
       while I start looking to the birds
outside our window, wishing they would
       beak right through, bird
me away. Me, the brilliant one who decided
       current events, sure,
guns, yes, my students finally want to talk,
       let them.
Guns are not the problem? How are they
       not? & my feet
want to stomp in agreement. My legs
       want to stand with
this student, her questions, not with the one who began
       her presentation, *Gun ownership*
is a basic American right, an important part of what makes
       our society free. & despite the impressive
lack of intonation, my chest wondered if
       she owned a gun, if
she ever carried in class, if I would notice, if she noticed
       during her five minutes

how I was trying not to be angry with her
        five minutes—my trying,
my face, she must've seen.
            Still she stood.
We are standing. & my chest tries to laugh
        a laugh that means, *This is serious, this
            is the class.*

a small book of questions: chapter ii

Can you describe a morning you woke without fear?

I walk to school. Everything bright & recognizable. Cactus plant. Dirty car window. This cloud. That. This dog bark. Those birdcalls. That boy in those shorts. These turquoise shorts I have on. I think, *Maybe I'll see that yellow bicycle again*, & I imagine seeing it & seeing the girl who dropped everything in the middle of the crosswalk, how quickly she had to move to get everything back in place, climb back on her yellow bicycle, 14 13 12, the crosswalk signal kept counting down, her instincts, 11 10 9, her movements, 8 7 6 5 4, as though nothing bad was happening, could ever, 3 2, happen.

How will you begin?

I reach campus. I pause in front of the library. *Wasn't I almost run over last night by a very large, very red truck?* I call a friend & say, *I'm on campus, now, yeah. So sweaty. Fall here's basically summer part two.* My friend says, *It's been warm in Chicago, too.* I pause on the phone, thinking, *on* the phone, not *in* the phone; *in* Chicago, not *on* Chicago, though you can write an article *on* Chicago. *You still there?* my friend asks. *Yeah.* I'm not sure how to broach my real subject, the reason I called. Is it rude to just blurt out to someone, *Hey, last night I almost died?* I then decide to ask my friend exactly that. & he replies, *Oh no,* &, *Wow,* & I feel uncomfortable feeling his sympathy. I think about calling my boyfriend. Shouldn't I tell him, too?

> I look around, as if someone might catch me in the scandalous act of thinking about my boyfriend. The library stands across from the Student Union Building. I consider the acronym, SUB, how it blends the words together into a kind of mush. SUB. A sandwich. I feel hungry. As the day goes on, everything gets more & more blended, sandwiched, together. The trees the clouds the turquoise the yellow sweat turquoise oh.

What are the consequences of silence?

I want to answer my mother: *No, I'm not afraid of women. & I'm not afraid of you. I love men. That's all. That's what you can't believe. Won't say. Won't let me answer, because you can't find the right question.*

Who was responsible for the suffering of your mother?

She says, *Please*. She says, *Call*.

My boyfriend says, *You should talk to your mother.* He reminds me that when his own mother was alive, he would talk to her every week. Implying: your mother is still alive;

you should talk to her every week.

My mother agrees with this premise. She calls me to explain why she called yesterday: *It was my birthday & no one was home. So I called you;*

I called your brothers.

My mother still has birthdays. She has phones. Land line, cell, she can call. She does. I don't pick up. I finally pick up. She says, *You should call.* My boyfriend nods. I hang up. I don't tell him she asks about the dog before she asks about him. In fact, she doesn't ask about him. She asks, *How is your dog doing? Has he grown very big now? Can you send me another picture? Is he fully trained now? How is he during walks?* She asks five questions about the dog. She says "he." She messes up his name but attempts his name.

I try to say, *So Jeff's been doing very well at work.* She says, *Oh, that's good.* I say, *Yes, & Jeff's the one who's been training the dog.* She says, *& how is school? How's your program going?* & I say, *It's good. I'm good. Happy*

birthday. I'm sorry I forgot to call.

Winter

You become increasingly indoorsy.

In the middle of cocoa & Tori Amos, you remember your mother calling back
     once—after you hung up on her.

She said, *You're just like me.*

Saying things you don't mean when you're angry.

At the time, you agreed with her, liked being like her, or that she thought, said
     you were.

This afternoon, you believe another nap will solve all your life problems.

When everyone knows naps are better suited for tackling geopolitics.

In a dream you try & fail at starting a dream journal, over & over.

Up again, you make tea, put on some Britney.

You stare out the kitchen window, out at the frozen yard, into the wind-faced
     hill—& you whisper, *Feel better.*

Then you think, you're saying, *No.*

I meant them. Not every word.

But every sound.

Elegy While Listening to a Song I Can't Help But Start to Move to

for Pulse

1.

What breaks me is their giddy, their swaying,
moments before.

2.

Yaeji sings *This product is called Depression*
& I think about how I haven't been out dancing
in a year, & how I say *Because I'm a homebody*
when my body misses the way bodies become song
& light.

3.

Their singing along, their jokes,
their swoon-worthy moves.

4.

How does a body forget all danger & become song, swoon?

5.

In the music video, Yaeji critiques makeup tutorials
by performing one. The makeup products are *ego, embarrassing moments,*
capital D *Depression.*

6.

How does a queer body—

7.

I'm in my 7th grade bedroom again, quietly
putting my hands on the warm hips of a tall
column of air. I've sculpted the air
into a boy:

Jake B. who
sits across in History.

I feel finally inside
my own face. I'm giddy. Then, afraid.

8.
Their clumsy-but-
don't-care, their beauty, the beauty of the night lit up
by a lyric, a kiss, some impossibly
impeccable hair.

Forgetting all danger because the lungs need to.
The legs.

9.
In the music video Yaeji dances
to the rhythm of her own satirical ritual, finding joy, or something like it.

10.
Their finding each other.

11.
What breaks.

12.
How sings a body.

13.
One night I walk by a soccer field & see
college boys playing, touching
each other rough, bare
chest meeting bright T-shirt shoulder,
& I can't help but think, sports
are super gay, think, the word "glistening"
must've been invented for just this sight, their moonlit

collisions, my instant replays
in slowest *cue the soft
music* motion.

14.

The body's truest thought is play, moon.

15.

How does my body—

16.

In the song another makeup product is *the unexpected tomorrow* Yaeji sings *Put on
the unexpected tomorrow* Yaeji sings & I sway, & yet.

Their laughter.

I keep hearing their laughter, moments before.

a small book of questions: chapter iii

How will you / have you prepare(d) for your death?

I kiss him. I kiss him.

a small book of questions: chapter iv

What do you remember about the earth?

The way sometimes he & I are clouds unable to touch, because he possesses a strange knowledge, the cruel knowledge that his mother is gone. The way sometimes he looks out into the trees, he said after his mother died he tried to feel her in the trees, in New York, & now the trees are different here, smaller, fewer. He wants my mother & me to talk. He wants to believe she is good, he believes I am, & I believe that, the way he turns to me. The way he says, *You.*

Who are you & whom do you love?

I tell him & he holds me. I tell him about the truck, its very large redness. He holds me & says, as he's said before, *We're both going to live to a hundred & then die peacefully in our sleep at the exact same time.* I say, *Yes,* I say, *Absolutely.* I kiss him, *Yes.* At the same time I think, But what about two hundred? Three?

What do you remember about the earth?

If we could communicate fully, there would be no need to communicate. If we could love perfectly, there would be no need to love. If we could finish grieving, there would be no need to live. If we could touch completely, there would be no need.

Who are you & whom do you love?

I know it can't be true, that although her favorite swearword in English is definitely "shit," my mother must've uttered, must've spat out the word "fuck" in more than one conversation, more than one argument we've had. But when I try to remember specific examples of times when my mother said "fuck," only one memory emerges: the time we were arguing about gay sex. As in, whether it was even sex at all. My mother kept saying, *That's just fucking.* At first I thought she was searching for the next word, that she was using "fucking" as a modifier for some horrible noun: fucking sickness, fucking madness, fucking filth. But then she went on: *That's just fucking; that's not anything.* She had found searches for gay porn in my Internet history. I had forgotten to erase them. I had forgotten

to forget them. *How can you look at that?*

She said "fucking" with such force, like she'd invented the word & was testing it out for the first time.

What do you know about dismemberment?

I write a poem about my mother's meat cleaver, which she uses to chop everything. I write a poem about my mother chopping watermelon. I write a poem about my mother crushing cockroaches with a shoe, a slipper, a roll of newspaper. I write a poem about my mother crying. A short poem about her arguing with my father. A longer poem about her wanting to boil him alive. A poem about her watching *Titanic* & hating the sad ending & saying, *I'm sick of sad endings.* A poem in which she is sick &, for a while, the doctors can't figure out why. I write a poem in which she has been dead for years. Five poems in which she doesn't die, she can't, will never. I start a poem in which she has a very long conversation with my boyfriend, then calls me to say, *I just had a very long conversation with your boyfriend, it & he were great!* I just can't figure out what would come next.

Who was responsible for the suffering of your mother?

I thought this time I'd write a book
just about my father.

a small book of questions: chapter v

How will you live now?

In other words, aren't both the triumphant & the tragic coming-out narratives white constructions, anyway? why do you need to talk to your mother about everything, anyway? does she need to be your best friend? was it failure,

> this fissure,
> or are you happier to have the space
> that opened up?

haven't you been happier, not speaking with her for almost a year?
would she wish to talk about your relationship, if you were with a woman?
is she just more interesting to write about than your father?
is it that she's shown more interest in changing? do you believe she'll get him
to change?

> or is it not space but distance?
> not happiness; relief?
> aren't you forgetting how you used to sit, after school,

at the kitchen table, & tell your mother every last thing from your day, the funny parts, the frustrating, the boys you liked to play Power Rangers with during recess, the boy you let play the Green Ranger, before you had to play Not Liking Boys No Not Like That, before you knew, before she knew, but didn't she, already?

One Year Later: A Letter

In memory of Christopher Andrew "Drew" Leinonen, 32, murdered with his boyfriend, Juan Ramon Guerrero, 22, in the shooting at Pulse, a gay nightclub in Orlando, June 12, 2016. It was Latin night at Pulse & many of the 49 victims, like Guerrero, were Latinx. Leinonen, one of the last to be identified, was Asian American. This poem addresses Leinonen as Drew because that was the name he chose for himself.

Dear Drew,

      I search your name again, find
a new picture of your mother.
Holding up the bright shirt

you died in. Looking at the holes, the bullet
holes. Waiting for one more gleam of you
to push through. Drew,

I didn't know you, but keep reading,
rereading about you. You
who shepherded friends & dates

& *maybe-I'm-not-100%-straights*
to their first gay club. You who danced
Dance Dance Revolution, watched

Star Trek, loved your
DVD collection. You who goofed,
giggled. You who shenaniganed. You who

all caps shouted *GAY*
like *YES* whenever someone tried
to lower case snicker, *are you…?*

You who worked as a counselor, who called
your red pick-up truck The Flamer, who donned
a floppy Santa hat for the gayest

holiday picture with your boyfriend & mother, you
who were dancing with your boyfriend, Juan,
then not, you who I keep reading

about until I keep seeing my face,
my brothers' faces
in yours, you who gleamed.

      Drew, sometimes I dream
into earlier that night, to the place
you shared with Juan.

You're getting ready
while he eats a snack in the kitchen.
You're trying on a blue shirt, thinking maybe

not. Then he comes in
to tease you for taking so long.
Juan, in his third

year of college & just weeks
away from his
twenty-third year. Juan,

the quieter one. Juan, fan of staying
at home, but also a fan
of Latin music, friends, dancing

with you. Juan, a big fan
of peanut butter. Juan who,
as one friend puts it, *was always trying to get*

everybody into peanut butter. Juan,
his hand
on your shoulder. Your hand,

his beardy cheek. Then him saying, *Yes,*
this shirt. Before the two of you
step out.

Drew, each time I dream it, I slow it down
a little more. You try on
five shirts. Each

with different shoes.
& Juan sits down to eat a whole
peanut butter sandwich.

Then another touch,
another touch
of his cheek.

      But sometimes, Drew,
there's another part of me, a not-small
part that returns

to your mother, instead of you.
The way she holds your shirt
with the largest missing.

Because I wonder, would my mother
do that for me?
My mother who once said, *If only I never*

had you. My mother who still can't say,
Your boyfriend. But knowing
my mother, I can say she would hold

it, even on the news, for everyone to see,
because a not-small part of her
would rather miss me

than listen to me,
listen to me say, again,
I love him.

      Drew, what did you say
to the unlistening? To the heart that prefers
a shineless shirt?

Summer

Your emergency contact has experienced an emergency.

The Texas sun shines hard on everything like a detective.

You hide out, eating every meal from microwavable cans.

Sometimes, you're studying abroad & ask the kitchen table where to find the
closest subway station.

Sometimes, the kitchen table replies, *By the family of cockroaches in the bathroom.*

Other times, *Language is the last thing you should learn more of.*

The cockroach family nods.

The Texas sky changes color like a vast PowerPoint very proud of itself.

You feel like a cockroach except you know how to use the microwave.

Sometimes, every living thing just sounds like: *Please.*

Other times, *Please don't. Please no.*

The mother cockroach says, *In the event of a sudden loss of cabin meaning, back-up
meanings will drop from the overhead compartment.*

The Texas moon shines like a misplaced clue.

Please grab hold of a meaning & pull it to your face.

Your kitchen table shines back, an unsolvable station.

Please hold, pull close.

a small book of questions: chapter vi

What do you remember about the earth?

beauty of west texas
sunsets, like creamsicles reaching their pinnacle, their final
evolution. beauty of every
dissertation title my friends invented every unfabulous
last week of a term. unbeauty of grading finals
while over-yet-still-under-caffeinated & clacking out
our own. beauty of queer texas
tech students forming a queer reading group.
beauty of a dry heat & everyone remarking *but at least
it's a dry heat.* beautiful
wind through trees whose beautiful names it took a year
to learn. bur oak, western soapberry, desert willow. hello,
beauties. undeniable beauty of
"of zombies & zest:
a queer poetics of *the walking dead's* steven yeun." undead
beauty of lubbock alleyways & their raccoons. beauty of those dauntless
dumpster divers. beauty of not
caring if the soul exists, so long as the heat of his inner thighs
does. beauty of caring
so much i handwrite a half-dozen cavafy poems i love,
while ignoring two paper deadlines. beauty
of him, & of he who licks
the sweat from my inner thigh. beauty of my ugly
handwriting. beauty of mitski, tweeting about caring
so much, saying, *fuck effortlessness. fuck that. try
really hard and let everyone
see.* beauty of writing poems
that former poetry teachers would not approve of—for example,
this one, which surely would anger the teacher
who said, *you overuse the word "beautiful"*
& the teacher who said, *never use the word "soul."*

beautiful beauty of the dry
soul of midday lubbock
beautifully, lubbockly unlocking every window.
beautiful anger
of a queer organizer, in the comment section of a poem
online, one of my lubbock poems. the organizer's beautiful
critique of my complaint
over how small lubbock pride was. her *you don't know*
how underfunded, understaffed we are. the beautiful back & forth
we were. beautiful,
to learn about her work, for her to learn about
my loneliness. beauty of our lonelinesses
talking. west texas beauty that some days hurt me into seeing
how much i missed my seasons,
my trees.
but beauty, the oddly
large dollhouse exhibit inside the massive windmill
museum. the beautiful fact that it is home
to more than 160 windmills. the beautiful, powerful wind
that made my beautiful, powerful bangs so unhappy.
exhausting beauty of trying to live
queer & asian, among so few of either, & were there ever
any of both?
yes, there was
one, a poet, who visited for a day. one gorgeously beautiful day,
beautiful regie cabico
on a texas tech stage, performing his poems. regie,
who had been invited by matthew, beautiful
lead organizer of the queer reading group, who another beautiful day,
invited me to a gathering around
my book. beauty of the invitation, beautifully crowded
discussion table. the red & black, unmistakably ttu conference room
queered by beautiful readers,
writers, beautified by queer makers
of t-shirts with lines from my poems, other poems, many.
queer beauty, glory of the group's questions,
our conversation—enthusiasms fabulousing the room.

& my handsomely beautiful pleasure-honor to say
how queer, isn't it, our living
here. how queer, west texas, thanks to us. how unfinal, our
unfurlings across the plains, our lines of pain, stanzas of standing
up. & then, on the t-shirt table, one beautiful,
beautiful, beautiful, beautiful
shirt, its pinkly
powerful shine—& the students saying, *go on!*
all yours! & i
sleep in it, now, back among the bursts of green, the long
new england grays i know so well. i fall
beautifully asleep in this shirt, nights when i miss their words,
that wind.

a small book of questions: chapter vii

What would you say if you could?

She asks about the dog before she asks about the boyfriend.

She doesn't ask about him. She does this for a year.

Will do this for years. Even after the boyfriend & I move back to the Northeast. Even when we're living ten minutes away & she comes to our apartment with an ugly vase I suspect she is regifting. I accept it because she has also brought a large container full of green beans fried with garlic. She looks at the dog, seems to have an easier time looking at the dog, than looking at the boyfriend, the boyfriends, us. I want to say, *Mom, look. Ask*

about us. She asks about the dog.

(How's his hair? Everywhere?)

Then I remember—about a year before we're ten minutes away, we come over from Rochester. We join my brother's college graduation lunch at Mu Lan in Waltham. & we're part of a party of six, eating as a party of twelve. The boyfriend goes to the bathroom. She goes back to the dishes, which are somehow not finished, yet. She's not. She's picking up two magnificently crispy scallion pancakes—their full magnificence held between her chopsticks, her skillfully nonchalant grip—& then she's placing them on the boyfriend's plate. She looks at me. Says, *For him.*

Maybe she is asking about us by asking about the dog.

> (Or she asks about the dog because he is cuter than the boyfriend, cuter than the son, we might as well all be regifted vases compared to the dog.)

She says, *He likes the pancakes, he should have more.*

& what would she say if she could

say, be more? & what am I looking for, exactly? Do I look at her, the way she would like? Have I said *I love you* recently—the exact words, yes, but what about the exact foods? Couldn't we ask each other for more?

At the least, I want to remember better. Earlier this summer, she asks if he's coming over with me, for the 4th. She's making hotdogs & hamburgers, wants to know if she needs to make veggie burgers. For the boyfriend. *For him.* For some reason I think dinner, not lunch, so say, *Sure, we'll both come once he finishes with work.*

She's disappointed when he can't come. She doesn't say disappointed. Says, *Take*

the veggie ones, & puts them in a large container, & that into a very large bag. Always these containers & bags, large & small & larger. She probably has something large enough, vast enough to carry all the hair the dog sheds, will ever shed.

> (I want to remember better.
> But I want more, more of the
> better to remember.)

She sighs in the midafternoon heat & I see the sweat on her face, then the lines.

Don't forget, she says, pointing to the bag with the veggie burgers. *For him.*

The School of Logic

I love you your Cheez-It-
       stained mouth. I love you
your legs, two furry examples
       of eternity. I love you your love
of instruction manuals, original
       packaging, the step-by-*Don't*
throw it out, don't you want to know
       how it works? I love you your logic,
your *Try it*. Your reaching
       for my hand again
in the South Plains Mall, Lubbock.
       Your flirty eyes in this A/C oasis
of mostly shoe stores.
       I don't love my refusing
to reach back.
       My logic of what if they spit, what if
fists. How I see
       every look. & think
we're too much love,
       even like, trying on shoes
side by side.
       How I can try on these clearly
gay sneakers, yet still leave
       A Buffer
between where I sit
       & you. How I've read
& never thrown out these instructions,
       their love
for telling me, *Under there, under*
       that under, that's where your family
           can see you.
But how I love you
       your seeing. Your grinning

Hey. Your soft *Come on,*
      hold my hand as we pass
the kiosk of aggressive
      T-shirt peddlers, the squawking
crew of college boys.
      Your *It's alright.*
Your *I'm here.* Your
      Fuck it & quick grip & before I
know it. Your logic
      more beautiful than mine.

The School of a Few or a Lot of My Favorite Things

My favorite season: horny during
a snowstorm. My favorite sad: sad while
watching ducks waddle about.
My favorite recent development: that ghosts prefer

to be called spooky babes.
Some of my favorite sunlights
include those that arrive in December
like gasps, like they've walked into a surprise

party, & they are the party, & it
is a ghost party.
Excuse me, a spooky babe party.
My favorite bedtime story: Once upon a time,

in a Chicago thrift store, I met the most stunning
purple blazer. My least favorite
any time story: Once upon a time, in a Boston area
laundromat, I remembered

middle school, all of it, & I couldn't stop
hating my hair. When did I start
loving my hair? My eyes?
Have I started?

I still think of him, that boy from that most
pimply, least favorite time. The boy
who walked through each seventh-grade classroom
tall & Swedish & American

& boy. He smelled like the dictionary definition
of blond. He could've been the definition
of popular. But was a total nerd. His favorites obscure
elf novels & obscurer German thrillers

& me. We walked
side by side through those halls.
Still, he could sit by his backyard swimming pool
like he was born there. A son of suburbia.

A babe. A favorite
sunlight & not just mine. & not
really mine, the way I hungered for,
hungering into his blue eyes, wishing

at him after he emerged from the blue,
all dripping blond bangs, all
dire loud pang
in my chest. Middle school,

wasn't that when I started to say I hate
math, stop the piano lessons, I'm not like the other
Asian kids, I'm not like
what they love?

Once upon a time, at dinner,
I told my mother to stop
making so much, why do you have to make
so much lu dou tang

all.
the.
time.
& she said, *I thought it was*

your favorite.
In school I kept saying, *I love writing*,
which I did, which I do,
which wasn't tall & Swedish & American

& American, but at least it wasn't math, Mozart,
the math of Mozart.

Years later,
earlier today, I said,

I'm a poet
as though saying, *Yes, really,*
I'm a person.
Once upon a time,

after school, I played Mozart. I played.
I didn't know I was a whole country's favorite
way to say somewhere
not real.

Or maybe I did know, but
not enough to stop
moving my hands across the keys.
Would I love the piano

now? Could I play
my favorites? Would I see my hands'
movement, my hands
as sunlight?

a small book of questions: chapter viii

What would you say if you could?

I imagine my mother sitting at home, sitting alone,
     no,
sitting surrounded by phones—on the wall, on the desk, on the kitchen table,
     in the watermelons,
     in the discarded egg shells,
     in the half-eaten fish saved in the fridge,
     in her hair,
     on her forehead,
     on her eyelid,
     in her blink,
     on,
     in,
     on,
     in,
     on,
     in,
          she is quiet, she has made herself quiet, so that if the smallest,
          tiniest snail of a phone
          rings, she'll hear it, she'll know
          how to receive the call.

What would you say if you could?

I imagine my mother in a red truck, her head
leaning out the window, her voice louder
than it's ever been, the volume is almost
too much:
     I'm sorry, I'm so sorry, I'm sorry, I didn't see you, it was so dark, I'm sorry, I
     made it that way, I didn't see, I didn't want to, I didn't see you, I couldn't see

     myself, I'm sorry, are you okay?

Origin Story

Night falls. Two other poets & I sit on the porch of a farmhouse in Tennessee. We eat two kinds of pasta, then gently shoo out two cats who like to wander in, often overstay. The one who has written the most this week is the best shooer.

I wish poets were named after their superpowers. Like, The Amazing Volta. Or, Captain Syllable Count. Or, Super Self Doubter.

One of the cats, I am told, gets fed at three houses. At each, he receives a different name. Simon is his name at the farmhouse & somehow, we agree to follow tradition, we pet him behind his ears & sing, *Simon.*

In college, a poetry professor asked, *Are you from Whitman or from Dickinson?* which sounded like he was asking, *Are you American?*

The next night, we find Simon sitting atop my bed. He won't budge. For a moment, he seems to look right at me, serious & exasperated, as though we'd come to an agreement weeks ago, about trading places, names, selves, & I'm the fool who's forgotten.

In one sense, I'm from Dickinson because I grew up two miles from her house, I grew up on afternoon field trips to her house, I close my eyes & I'm standing in her house, the well-practiced tour guide singing, *I like to see it lap the Miles — And lick the Valleys up —*

How fourth-grade me thought she was talking about a giant cat.

Rain falls. I press my head against a foreign pillow. It's too green. I try to sleep, to let my mind leave me & then, reenter.

In the tingly hairy gay sense, I'm from Whitman.

In the refusal of sense, I'm from the cat we agree to call Simon. I'm from his other names. I'm from his future names. I'm from the hunger between his names. I'm from the wet grass he walks through to reach the next house.

Winter

It's April.

But still cold. Could still snow. Because that's what Massachusetts does.

What do I do? Sleep too much. Too little. Write nothing.

Except another tweet about another article about the rise of hate crimes against Asians & Asian Americans. A text to a friend. This list of five things I love, in no particular order: Oak trees. Men's calves. Honey oolong milk tea with boba. The interrobang. A video in which a young Björk says, *You shouldn't let poets lie to you.*

J. always sleeps too little.

It's April & where are the tests?

In one dream I get to go to the boba tea place & I get a house-sized serving of honey oolong milk tea with boba. It's difficult to carry back to the apartment, but I manage.

I cry, some nights. J. holds me, says, *I'd eat a bag of your hair*—a code we developed one long ago night when I asked him, *Would you eat a bag of my hair?*

It's April, I'm telling my students, *It's going to be okay.*

I tweet about a white checkout boy who is handing a receipt to a customer, who sees me in line, who demands I step back, wait behind the red x on the supermarket floor. I thought it was my turn, apologize. Then while I'm still waiting, a white man crosses the red, steps up right behind me. The boy says nothing.

It's April. Where are the tests?

Maybe I should delete the tweet about the white checkout boy & the white man

& the red x. Was it racism? It wasn't getting spat on. Kicked. Punched. Spat on spat on spat on. It wasn't an acid attack. But, it wasn't a coincidence.

J. holds me, says, *I'd eat three bags of your hair.*

It's April & the air tastes like rain remembering snow. A student asks what to do when you're stuck. I suggest a list. I always suggest a list. *Here*, I say, *I'll do it at the same time as you.*

Another list of five things I love: Magnolia trees. Men's nipples. The sea (not swimming in it, just being by it). The night sky (looking up into it, feeling of it). Lists (lying about how they're in no particular order).

It's April & what the fuck?

I consider Trump's lies vs. mine. The government's lies vs. the people's. Was my student asking about being stuck in her writing or in 2020?

I tweet about a white cook working in a banh mi food truck refusing to give me a box for my banh mi after seeing my hands on the still-wrapped sandwich. I tell him, *The wrapping's not enough; I'm taking this on a long subway ride back home.* He says, *We're not supposed to touch the food again* & expresses concern for my safety. Then hands a white customer's order back to her in the box she asked for. Smiles at her. She smiles back.

Another list of five things I love, in very particular order: Cherry trees. Men's musky armpits. Lies that are my backstory of how exactly Björk came to distrust poets, then used an e.e. cummings poem as lyrics for one of my favorite shorter songs of hers. The way I don't care if heaven exists, so long as men's musky armpits do.

The smallest words, I tell my students, *can make a world of difference. Conjunctions like "but," "and," "or." Adverbs like "then."*

How often "then" occurs in scenes like at the food truck—the lie the cook tells me, the truth he smiles at her, the reality that depends on the lie that there is only one, pure truth.

It's April & when am I going to giggly-hug my friends, again?!?

Every time I see "Kung Flu" on Twitter, I make a note to get another honey oolong milk tea once Kung Fu Tea reopens.

It's April & I would eat three bags of J.'s hair, too.

Though lately can't stop thinking about how he isn't the one whose food these other white men won't touch.

I make a list of the white men I've dated, hooked up with, wanted. It's a long list.

It's almost May & why are all the Chinese American friends I want to guffawly-hug in New York, on the West Coast?!?!

I want to write about snow. Instead of my list of white men. Then realize I usually write "silver" to describe snow, instead of "white." The moon, too. "Silver" or "golden." & any bright light—just "bright." The fact that I can't write "white" without thinking of my list of white men. Of my first boyfriend, his bright white teeth as he said, *I like your eyes, they're not really chinky eyes*. The way I said, *Thank you*.

Or my third boyfriend, how he liked to call my dick an eggroll, proudly called himself a rice queen.

All the ways I said, *Thank you*.

Or all the dates with white men where I was just elated they didn't call themselves rice queens. Or the white professor who didn't call himself a rice queen but was always seen with younger Chinese men. Or the white professor who was always seen with younger Chinese men but didn't call himself a rice queen. How I was the younger man, had trouble calling myself Chinese.

The fact that I can't write about the snow without writing about standing in it, still as a tree, wishing it would cover my entire body in a thick blanket of white, white, white.

To realize some of my writing is just my saying to white men: Look how lovable I am.

How I've thought that being with a white man would whiten me, lighten my lonely. & actually, factually, being with some white men has blanketed me while covering me in lonelier.

The fact that I love J. for J.

Just as this country does. Most of this country does, before learning he has a boyfriend. What percentage of this country loves me, after reading my name, after seeing my face, after hearing me talk about my boyfriend?

After a list of your loves, I tell my student who's feeling stuck, perhaps in every possible way, *make a list of your questions*. Like:

What is love? Is it just saying *I'll eat a hundred bags of your hair*? Or is it also talking, continuing to talk about the fact of his whiteness, my notness? How it is that I am an antonym for person, synonym for sickness? This one & a myriad before & mutations to come?

Is posing all this as a set of questions when I already know the answers a form of lying?

Sure.

It's May, I need this form of lying.

In order to spell the facts out. In order not to fall under the facts of the particular order of the world as is. In unordered love.

In another dream I get to go to my favorite restaurant in Los Angeles. Which somehow is also my childhood apartment in Western Mass. There's the sporty smell of my boyhood shampoo. There's no food. Nevertheless, everyone's seated at big wooden tables with blue linen tablecloths. Chatting away. The clink of champagne glasses, but no champagne, not one glass. & in the background, the beep-burps of dialup Internet, with no bulky Dell computer in sight.

Mostly, it's Chinese people. Chinese & Chinese American. Some of them with non-Chinese partners. Some of them queer. Some of them with my face; I mean, at least five of them literally have my face. I sit down next to one. His eyes—my eyes. He smiles. Not my smile, or not yet.

In the World's Italianest Restaurant

in memory of Justin Chin, 1969–2015

OK but why aren't more people talking about the fact—the undeniably
indisputable fact—that you were hot?

A simple Google image search confirms this. My erogenous zones
affirm this. You with your

tattooed arms, which clearly you knew were A Key Feature, yes I'm talking
about all those photos

in a plain T-shirt, polo, tank top. You with your goatee & mustache,
the stache I'm trying

these days to emulate. Did you ever go full-on caterpillar with that?
Did it work—meaning,

was it hot? These are the questions I need to ask you. If only
we'd met. I wish we could meet,

this bright blue afternoon, in the boba tea shop down the street, the spot
I always ask folks to come to,

even from the afterlife, or what must be the bluest of oblivions.
But if you're feeling

fancy, let's go to that Pizza Hut, the one my aunt took me to once, in Xiamen,
& let me tell you—

stunning. Like a seriously *Italian* Italian fine dining establishment.
I'd order us a large

pepperoni pizza, then between bites tell you about the white guy on Facebook
who called me an "identitalian clown"

for posting "nonstop" about race. I'd write a poem called "White Guys on Facebook"
but I'd rather not further exhaust

my exhaustion. How tired were you? Growing up?
In those last years?

Some days I wonder if I'll make it to your age.
46.

Scrolling down the same image search, the cover of my first book
pops up,

from an article about Asian American poets. *Gutted*
is highlighted, your

last book of poems. I wish I could've sent you my first. & told you
what it felt like to find yours,

Bite Hard, in a college library. The way I hid it
between two more

innocent-looking books I've long since forgotten. This habit I began
in high school—sneaking

into my backpack, then my room, all the queer
lit, every bit of this

aliveness I could find. The fact—the fact I'd love to dispute, deny,
but can't—that it took

until college to find books & writers both queer & Asian.
How I'm still shedding

the unaliveness, the lie that queer & Asian must mean un- & never-
innocent, that to live

like you is to choose pain & sorrow
& pain.

Have you heard about this new virus? That a body like yours, like mine
is once again presumed sick,

preferred dying, pronounced tragic-
ally already dead?

I wish, I need to: send you this poem. Or better: for us to write
together, to compose an acerbic yet ecstatic

epic called "Identitalian Clowns" that recounts every moment of the bright
afternoon we ate pizza, while talking

about how painful this world has made our living—
as well as how hot & mustachioed

& hot
we can't help but continue to make ourselves.

Summer

The sunflowers fall, right along with their mason jar, in the middle of the night. Their heads too gloriously full of early July. How they seem to know everything, except the virus. The crown it wears. All the unglory it craves. Receives.

/

At Williams Sonoma the other day, a sales associate named Carol welcomes the two of us to a new, touchless shopping experience. It's a capacious Williams Sonoma, at the Natick Mall, & we're impressed by how Carol's voice fills the entire store. Her cheery script a lingering chime in our ears. We're here after our usual supermarket trip, curious how the mall is reopening. & Carol—I know she's paid to sound happy about this situation, as she's paid to ooze happiness about every Le Creuset skillet, kettle, cassoulet. But she sounds far too happy.

\

Something wakes the dog. His barking like fistfuls of sunlight, like the sun set on fire. I sit up at once, understand what he can't: the sunflowers, the jar, on the carpet. You groan, slowly raise your right hand, the only part capable of any semblance of awake. You caress the dog's head. His back.

You soften the fright away with syllable after syllable of your hand.

/

I wave to Carol as though sending her some love, though mostly it's concern. She smiles & smiles, as though the smile has kidnapped her, as though her name isn't actually Carol, as though Williams Sonoma has given her that name, taken all her vocabulary except smiling & *How may I assist you??*

\

I keep seeing it in slow motion, though I didn't actually see their falling. The sunflowers, overcome with true dizzying delight—with themselves.

/

I miss seeing your delight when touching pots & pans & potato mashers, the vast array of Le Creuset. That afternoon with one autumnally orange Dutch oven. Your face, as you touched that fire. Your face whenever you just have to touch the fabric of every shirt that catches your eye in H&M, tell me exactly how it feels. Then ask me to touch it, describe it myself. So soft, yes, but in what way? Like a cloud? About to burst?

\

I picture Carol with sunflowers.

In a Williams Sonoma-approved apartment, Carol is allowed one sunflower, one real happiness she can put in her own jar.

/

Your hand doesn't touch even the shirts now, though you read somewhere fabrics are okay, the virus can't live on them, or not for long, or what are the facts, today?

\

Or perhaps Carol, when she's not a grinning retail robot, is the patron saint of sunflowers.

The pricey cookware, just her day job.

/

I miss museums. Walking around with you, coming across an exhibit that exclaims, Touch me! Watching your fingers revel in being fingers on a wacky new surface.

Then kissing you hard while that twelve-foot tall papier-mâché duck watches, jealous.

Let there be a patron saint of making impossible birds very annoyed.

\

July 7, 2020: Over three million confirmed cases in the US. Over fifteen thousand in critical condition. Over one hundred & thirty-three thousand dead. Over half a million dead globally.

/

Many of the things I miss are pretty silly. Pretty & silly. & I miss them deeply.

& my mother, who lives only ten minutes away by car, but hasn't left the house in months, has insisted I not leave mine unless absolutely necessary. My mother, already sick, chronically sick in three different ways. She says not to send anything. How I want to send her all the sunflowers.

Carol, you may assist me now. If you are indeed the holy rep of sunflowers, Carol—please make row after row flicker up in the night, in the worry-field of my mother's head. Help her sleep. & dream only of glowing, petal-soft things.

\

Surely, there is a patron saint of touch, who yes, at the moment is struggling—unlike the brand-new patron saint of branded touchless experiences, whose business has only been expanding. Booming, like a dog's 3 a.m. holler.

/

I miss walking through a museum by myself. That sweet surrounded-by-art aloneness. Solitude enhanced, perfected—by unwearable pantsuits, hairy suitcases.

I think it's what any artist hopes for: not only to be remembered, but to be company.

\

Perhaps Carol really is overcome with joy. Thrilled, like us, to be out of the apartment, away from her relentlessly beautiful dog, cat, kid. Even when it means repeating the same couple of lines, a sort of depressing jingle. & the mask—all day. Still, she's out & she's caroling about the latest sale on summer grilling essentials. To people who—perhaps she's glad for it—don't know her.

/

They fell? you ask in the morning, surprised to see the sunflowers strewn on the carpet. *Yes*, I say, & explain how that led to the dog barking. I add something about being too lazy to pick them up, but really, I liked the way they looked on the carpet, like golden messages from some other, less exhausting place.

You pick the sunflowers up, return them to their jar after refilling it with fresh tap water. You climb back in bed & touch my face.

You climb back in bed to touch my face.

You wrap your arms around me & it's like you're the patron saint of touch as well as soft sunlight & soothed dogs. Or you must be the earthly representative of divine holding. Or you're both & also a boy, like me, holding on.

Things the Grackles Bring

An eggy disaster. An opulently abandoned theatre. A jade box of childhood
fears. A library book overdue & despised. A highway
beautification with a rerun of the full moon. An infomercial
they would really like us to watch, in formalwear. Their aunties

who each bring just a thimble of thunder. Their grandmothers
who bring us geodes to crack: a jack, a jenny. Twins!
Reasonably priced dental plans! Fondue & dipping breads
but we're already full. Other birds but we don't care about them. Words

we've spoken to our parents that we would take back. That we wouldn't.
The blue pen that exploded. What bees wear at night
when they want to feel sexy. The math of Halley's Comet. A miracle
but we just couldn't accept, no no, that's far too much, you're too kind, no.

Jasmine tea. Property tax. War but they see our hands
are already full of it. So. The notion that if we mourned every single person
killed just today. Learned the name & wept the name.
If we had the body. To grieve every body.

They bring it to our doorstep.

After My White Friend Says *So Cool* Upon Hearing Me Speak Chinese on the Phone with My Parents, I Take Another Sip of My Strawberry-Banana Smoothie & Contemplate Coolness & Chineseness, I Wonder If My Love of Long Titles Stems from the Long Titles of Classical Chinese Poets & Is, Therefore, Part of an Inherently Cool Chineseness I Have Inherited, & Carry, Even to the Smoothie Shop, & Then I Recall a Longish Stream of Not-So-Cool Things My Parents Have Said About White People

他为什么生气？

她不会吃辣，别给她太多。

他们的电影很奇怪。

我的 supervisor, 她送的 email 都很长，没时间都慢慢读。

他疯了。

她要问我什么？

你应该跟老中 together。

太麻烦！

我们讲中文，他们老是想我们在讲他们的事，可是我们不在乎。

她为什么这么不耐烦？

她是不是你的女朋友？你们两个老是有空 hang out, 聊天。

But that doesn't make sense.

他不喜欢吃米饭，应该给他 pizza。

见鬼!

他们的电影很奇怪，大家老是很伤心，我不知道为什么。

He wants us to 帮他搬 a 钢琴？

他们两个是不是 together?

她会不会帮你？

你为什么喜欢 boys？你不知道怎么喜欢 girls？

你可以跟老美 together。

你学习必须努力。

你不需要跟他们比。

你需要比他们写的更好。

你要不要去看 La La Land？

他们不需要像我们这样天天 work。

我没空。

Every Poem Is My Most Asian Poem

Including the poems I have yet to write.
For example, the one about the two
gray pubes, discovered during last Tuesday's

trim. Or, the one about the fourth
hedgehog of the post-apocalypse. Or, the long,
tragic one about how the frenemy of your frenemy

is your frenemy. The short one that seems
to be about love, but is about
SUNY Geneseo. The one about my best friend who always

mistakes everyone for Anne Carson,
tentatively titled, "Why Canada Cannot Stop
Weeping." Of course,

there's the one that begins, *Exquisitely
inquisitive, I wander with my well-moisturized elbows.*
& ends, *To aubergine or not to aubergine, that is*

never the question. This great poem I will
never write, for I am too busy staring
at my graying or correcting my best friend. & in the end,

I only know the beginning & the end. Everything else
is a superlative question—a supervoid
I have come to view as my innermost joy.

I am reminded via email to resubmit my preferences for the schedule

But really
I would prefer
to sit, drink water,
reread some Russians
awhile longer
—a luxury
perhaps, but why
should I, anyone,
call it that, why
should reading
what I want,
in a well-hydrated fashion,
always be what I'm
planning to finally
do, like hiking
or biking, & now
that I think of it, reading
should make me, anyone,
breathe harder, then
easier, reach for cold,
cold water, & I
prefer my reading
that way, I prefer
Ivan Turgenev,
who makes me work for
not quite pleasure
no, some truer
sweatier thing,
Turgenev,
who is just now,
in my small room
in West Texas,

getting to the good part,
the very Russian part,
the last few pages
of "The Singers"
when the story
should be over,
Yakov the Turk
has sung with fervor,
meaning true
Russian spirit,
meaning he's won
a kind of 19th century
Idol in the village
tavern, The End, but
Turgenev goes
on, the narrator walks
out, down a hill,
into a dark
enveloping mist,
& he hears
from misty far away
some little boy
calling out for
Antropka!
calling hoarsely,
darkly,
Antropka-a-a!
& it's that voice that stops
then opens my breath
that voice
& all Monday-Wednesday-Fridays
all Tuesday-Thursdays
are gone
I have arrived
in the village of
no day   none
& I am sitting

with the villagers
who are each at once
young   old
who have the coldest
water to give me
& songs
I think I have sung   before
they sing
their underground
tree-root syllables
they give me silences
from their long
long   hair

four short essays personifying a future in which white supremacy has ended

1.

                                        therefore,

2.

i walk, chewing bubblegum, which should make
a happy feeling, bubbly me   but,

i am busy considering
how to personify
is to make a person out of feelings

& not necessarily to make
more personable   again,

i tap on the window of feeling
unseen & the window
refuses to personify me   see,

some people are not yet personified
while trees often are & the birds

in poems & the pets
of white people most often   &,
the present refuses to personify into a future

of bubbly walking   yet,
to person is to feel, & necessary   so,

i read a friend's poem
in which the word "emotionality" feels
out for me in the middle of our unseen   in fact,

i feel the word sounds clunky   then again,
aren't actual feelings

clumsy, & within our unbubbly
i sound out a clumpy, a cracked   exhaling,
i will feel

3.

so healed when white people
finally shut up
about that one time they went to asia

& felt so spiritual & healed
for poetry should not be therapy,

poets say, though still i feel
that some would prefer me
to therapize

them with yummy feelings
of migrant tragedy, fix them

up a fixed dictator-&-
dumplings past,
never to walk into a future

of unpersonable feelings

for to feel is to window

& to person is to people
a feeling, a future
in which

4.

this future walks,

unpersonifiable, because

what, who

is a person

in these windows, now

Chen   No Middle Name   Chen

[an anagram poem using only the letters in the title]

called Chad   called homo
called mini   and ma'am
called no man   called Chinaman
        am I a man?

once on a coach   a man called me
Anne   claimed I had   a nice
Mom 'do   and needed
        a hand

call me   odd   call me
mean   I am   no
calm   clean nod   amen
        I am

Chen middle name Oceanic   middle name
Alchemic   middle name Moon Ode   Eel Dance   Oh Damn

The School of Song, Uno, & Dinnertime

My song is snow in March,
in May. My song is eighty degrees
the next day. My song couldn't decide
what to get you, so here,
everything. My song, the sky
over Amherst, Massachusetts.
My song goes, *Happy birthday,*

Emily Dickinson. My song goes on
field trips to Emily's house & books
& dress & funky gift
shop & tour guides who once worked
for the post office & now work for her
light. My song wants to stand as tall
as a former postal worker

standing in the middle of Emily's room
& singing, *The Soul selects her own Society —*
Then — shuts the Door —
But tonight, from across
the country, my song is a different
selection. My song wants to open the glass
sliding door of the kitchen

of my parents' house
outside Boston, where we moved,
where they must be now,
this November night,
making soup with fish balls, & fried rice
with leftover everything. My song sees
my parents, their shoulders bumping

in that small kitchen. My song hears Dad's sigh,
Mom's *Shit* when they see

they're out of vinegar. My song is how
they're improvisers. My song,
my brothers, both home
from college, sliding slipper-footed
into the kitchen, & hungry.

My song wants to say, *I know I haven't
called*, say, *I'm still angry, but
should call*. My song is trying
to tell my brothers, *I'm angry, but
not with you*, you who
last December gave me the gift
of a shrug, of saying, *That's great*

when I told you about the man
I love. My song is the way we jumped
right back to a brutal round of Uno
& I was too bowled over by the two
of you to even try saving myself. Or to tell you
that my song was, for years, Dad's
Never tell any other family, Mom's *Never tell*

your brothers. My song was one long note
of *Never*—the door shut
before I could select all of my society.
& then the teacher,
the white teacher I thought would listen
to all of the song, how he said, *Is it
because of their culture? Just so behind*

the times? How he would take his time
to speak of Whitman & Dickinson, to sing
each line just so,
just so. My song, the wind
in my face. This song, *I'm still angry, but.*
Your song,
my brothers, your ferocious

laughter, when I lost to you, when I didn't
lose you. & our parents—
would you believe I miss them, too?
That tonight, I'm hearing
their shoulders, bumping? Their hands
placing bowl after bowl of garlicky
light on the kitchen table.

Their shoulders, their elbows,
as one squeezes past the other, dashes
from kitchen to foot of the stairs, & calls
for you. You know—*Come on! It's getting cold!*
Their calling you by name,
by full *It's dinnertime!* name. *Come on,*
while it's still warm—

One Year Later: Her Answer

in memory of Ruthann Johnson

September, again
& she is

not, again
& he keeps thinking of things to ask her
then remembering he can't, & I could

ask, in a beautiful
poem sort of way, what was the creature she always wanted

to growl as, the candy she always hoped
to create? But I want him to be able to pick up the phone, to call
his mom with all his beautifully

boring questions—yeah, it's the fridge again, what
should I do? What should I check first?

Should I take everything
out? Just put it on the floor? Are you home,
are you watching *Frasier*?

But the last question I can remember, the one I keep remembering
her answer to

was in the hospital. & I can't stop hearing, seeing
her voice, her face in the hospital,
when the social worker came, asked if everyone in the room

was family—when his mother, from her bed, looked
right at me, said, *Yes.*

The School of Keyboards & Our Whole Entire History Up to the Present

Hi 琛
—your text wakes my phone & I can see
the moments before your sending: thumb hovering, potential characters
having popped up after you switched

keyboards, typed "Chen." 琛—you're one of a few who write it, say me
like that. You write It's been a long time & it feels like the question

behind the statement—why
haven't we talked? So busy I reply, when part of me
wants to call, say *I miss you,*

Mom. To speak that sentence in Mandarin. It's been a long time
since I've spoken any Mandarin, any
to you. Some days I forget my name
isn't just "Chen." Worry I'll forget how to write it, without my phone, without

you to write it to. What do you still need to finish this semester? you ask
& I almost laugh—it's a question you've asked me

since conception. How different is it now, in PhD land? Might as well be back
in high school, scrambling to finish French
sentences about shopping on the Champs-Élysées

while aboard the shivery bus, or in the chattery cafeteria, lunch tray
balanced atop my knees. I was young. I said *Here*
I am. Do you have any idea how often
they called me strong, they said *I don't know how you do it, you're so*

brave & strong? Friends, classmates, teachers,
counselors, cafeteria ladies: Hi, SoBrave&Strong! as they passed in the hall.

Because I was young & said *Here I am*. While you said *Wrong,*
Wrong. While guys on the track team laughed & laughed because *Hey,*
French earlier, wasn't it so

gay? While girls I just met linked arms with me, paraded
me around. While teachers applauded me for becoming
president of the GSA,
then never attended another meeting. While my best friends

& favorite grownups spent their lunches listening, their free blocks listening.
They knew nobody is SoBrave without anybody's &,

somebody else's Strong—why didn't
you? Why couldn't I tell you about the boy
who dumped me via his away message on AIM? Or the boy who demanded

I have "anime hair"? Or the one who kept saying you were *Horrible,*
a horrible mother & I said
Yeah, & kept sipping my lukewarm chai, & later asked When can I see you
again? & he said Yeah

I don't think we really clicked & I don't blame him, I brought up
my whole entire history with you on the first date, I mean, why

did your name for me
also have to be SoBrave&Strong, why not
just Loved?

I know,
it's been years since you've said *Wrong.*
But you still haven't said Happy Anniversary! Six years, wow!
—what I hoped for last week.

Some days I imagine a different history. Us
talking. If only I could've told you

about high school,
about college. & you could've said *Come here. At home*
you don't have to worry about that.

Imagine it: me coming home, me running to you
to rant about a boy, & you shaking your head, *That boy? All wrong*
for you anyway. If only you'd say *How right,*
this boy, taking good care of you now.

OK I have to get this work done, but I'll
call you soon—I don't know whether that sentence, either part,

is true. Whether I'm lying. My thumb hovers, considers
switching keyboards. To ask Are you ready now, 妈?
妈妈?

Autumn

Autumn approaches
and the heart begins to dream—

— Bashō, tr. Sam Hamill

My heart comes back in a very large FedEx box.

As though it has accumulated many new possessions.

But no, it is just surrounded by a lavish amount of bubble wrap.

Kneeling on the carpet, I lift it out.

& feel for a moment like I've won a raffle, though I don't recall buying a ticket.

Then I bring my heart up to my face.

& find it giving off a mystery odor.

Like a relative you want to have to buy a bus, no, plane ticket to see.

Yet this pounding is, undeniably, me.

Demanding a flawless performance of the entire *Lion King* soundtrack.

Asking, does the moon ever get sad?

Needing to know, does the moon get terribly sad because it is simply called
the moon, & not some fancy Greek name, like the myriad moons of
Jupiter, like Callisto, for example, from the Greek kallistos, superlative
form of kalos, meaning "beautiful"?

Then, knowing:

The moon does not get sad. Or at least, not because of that.

Of that, the moon is terribly proud.

IV

I Invite My Parents to a Dinner Party

In the invitation, I tell them for the seventeenth time
(the fourth in writing), that I am gay.

In the invitation, I include a picture of my boyfriend
& write, *You've met him two times. But this time,*

you will ask him things other than can you pass the
whatever. You will ask him

about him. You will enjoy dinner. You will be
enjoyable. Please RSVP.

They RSVP. They come.
They sit at the table & ask my boyfriend

the first of the conversation starters I slip them
upon arrival: *How is work going?*

I'm like the kid in *Home Alone*, orchestrating
every movement of a proper family, as if a pair

of scary yet deeply incompetent burglars
is watching from the outside.

My boyfriend responds in his chipper way.
I pass my father a bowl of fish ball soup—*So comforting,*

isn't it? My mother smiles her best
Sitting with Her Son's Boyfriend

Who Is a Boy Smile. I smile my Hurray for Doing
a Little Better Smile.

Everyone eats soup.
Then, my mother turns

to me, whispers in Mandarin, *Is he coming with you*
for Thanksgiving? My good friend is & she wouldn't like

this. I'm like the kid in *Home Alone*, pulling
on the string that makes my cardboard mother

more motherly, except she is
not cardboard, she is

already, exceedingly my mother. Waiting
for my answer.

While my father opens up
a *Boston Globe*, when the invitation

clearly stated: *No security*
blankets. I'm like the kid

in *Home Alone*, except the home
is my apartment, & I'm much older, & not alone,

& not the one who needs
to learn, has to—*Remind me*

what's in that recipe again, my boyfriend says
to my mother, as though they have always, easily

talked. As though no one has told him
many times, what a nonlinear slapstick meets

slasher flick meets psychological
pit he is now co-starring in.

Remind me, he says
to our family.

ode to my beloveds & brevities

& beautiful jorts & beautifuler
pug breaths & the best of sandra
bullock & a slice of watermelon bursting
between the teeth of a boy in a bathtub
in an unmistakably ren hang photograph & you
are back home & you
are my favorite unabridged
absurdity & you
& i & why don't we start in this bed
the next big greater boston sandra
oh fan club & yes let's think
trees in late december
while we embrace & yes believe
them to be an abundance
of baldnesses & no
two the same & every one a blast & a half
& another half & the last poem i tried to write about
our no longer puppy but
always our baby just went like
!!
& with a jiggly leap into the bed here he is
& what could be more
breathgiving than these pugly (meaning
beautifulest) wrinkles & nostrils &
couldn't we just gobble
up our little never bashful
buddy's ears
but wait i'm not supposed to say that
with my chinese breath
but (& eternally) fuck that
isn't this a fantabulous day & isn't his smile very
dog & aren't the three of us the busiest
goofballs & the strangest heartthrobs

& the gabbiest unstrangers &
some abracadabra mixed
with kablooey & unbamboozled
except by each other & fantabulously
pugly & oh
& so & gobbleable & &
& &
&
& & & & &
& why should we ever leave this bed
or these breaths

我疼你

1.

Don't you get out of my hair, 爸, don't you stop
your big sneeze ways, your boogers of 爸 truth
flying across the kitchen, skipping right over a pot of soup
to which you've just added your chili flakes, then out
the sliding glass door, across
the city, to land in the unruly field
of my bangs, where they've always
belonged, bless you. Don't you stop loving me, 爸. This
& all your ways.

Don't you get out of my teeth, 妈, don't you leave
my teeth so sadly
spinachless, your mega-green
strands of 妈 knowing & wise
ribbing stuck in this abundance of crooked
teeth, thank you. Don't you
stop loving me, either.
Never. This, 妈, & every way
of yours.

2.

爸妈, don't you stop giving me
grief, but don't you ever (I know) make me (I know) grieve
you (it's impossible
not to, one day).

3.

爸妈, 我疼你——how is it now my turn to say it to you?
Except really
about you, & to other people, just as I'm sure
you've said it. This way. To closest friends.
To your 爸妈.
我疼他.

我疼他们, I want to say to my closest
about you. The two of. The 疼
that taps on my shoulder, tugs me by the ear
to our history again.
Again, your faces
in my words.

4.

疼 as in ache. pain. pang. your faces. 疼
as another way to say 爱,

我疼你 as another way to sing 我爱你,
but pangfully,

like an ache in my most crooked tooth,
song of my longest hair.

5.

疼, to tend, to be tender, to attend
each other's lives. 疼 as in our lives have hurt
each other—why?

疼 as in the wish to become another world
for you, far away

from this world
that imagines (when did you know) you,
prefers (that imagination could wreck) you

a thing, wishes you
& me dead.

6.

疼, which contains 冬,
which means winter.
Likely a sonic borrowing, since 疼 is téng, 冬 is dōng—

probably, at an earlier time, they lived closer
in sound. Winter, living

beneath the roof-like 疒 radical, meaning "sickness."
To be sick in the heart of winter. No.
To be sick with a winter's heart. No.
To be sick with winter for you—is that the love
I feel? A perpetual inner

December? Does to love mean to worry, to be a worrier
on the snowy field of another's face?
Once, you said you were worried
I'd get my brothers, your other (truer?) sons, sick.
More than once. The both of you. Said. This.

Sick with what, neither of you could say
out loud. *Get out before you get them sick, too.*
& now the country we live in believes everyone with a face
like ours is sick. Our sick faces, sick countries, *go back
before you get us sick.*

7.
Winter,
in a word that means shield & shattered, roof
& rain, a love that hurts to give,
receive. Have I wanted
to hurt you back? Did my poems
hurt you? Do I want these words to wound?

8.
疼, a family, tending
to each other's history—is this tenderness, such 疼

possible? 疼, I want to see its roof-
like 疒 radical as a roof over us, & we're warmed, warming
up to each other again. For now, the 疼 we have, are: a December

ache, windy
loving, this don't you stop 冬天 field
full of my to-you,

for-you words, 爸, my shivers, 妈, tender
as snow & silver as falling.

The School of Night & Hyphens

The sky tonight, so without aliens. The woods, very lacking
in witches. But the people, as usual, replete

with people. & so you, with your headset, sit
in the home office across the hall, stuck in a hell

of strangers crying, computers dying, the new
father's dropped-in-toilet baby

photos, the old Canadian, her grandson Gregory,
all-grown-up-now Greg, who gave her this phone

but won't call her. You call her
wonderful. You encourage her to tell you what's wrong

with her device. You with your good-at-your-job
good-looking-ness, I bet even over the phone

it's visible. I bet all the Canadian grandmas
want you, but hey, you're with me. Hey, take off

that headset. Steal away from your post. Cross
the hall, you sings-the-chorus-too-soon, you

makes-a-killer-veggie-taco, you
played-tennis-in-college-build, you Jeffrey, you

Jeff-ship full of stars, cauldron full of you,
come teach me a little bit

of nothing, in the dark
abundant hours.

Ode to Rereading Rimbaud in Lubbock, Texas

In the armpit of summer. In the asshole of August. In the what-the-fuck-am-I-doing of more grad school. I am in the 20th grade, rereading Rimbaud's "Sonnet du Trou du Cul," co-authored with his often-fucked-up sometimes-boyfriend Verlaine. Their joint ode to the asshole. The literal hole, puckering. The literal hole, the surrounding hairs. The metaphorical lips, & hunger. In Lubbock, Texas. In Jesus saves & Buddy Holly rocks. In *Guns up!* & *Ah, that line break!* In recently voted second most conservative city in the country. In the year marriage equality is made the law of the land. In the year the law is laughed at, spat on, called a sign of the end. I reread the sonnet, the ode, then go, inspired, horny, to the one I love. Tongue in armpit in asshole tongue on cock on cock tongue in love. My poetics of deepthroat & tonguefuck. I love my poetics. From the French: *la mousse humide encore d'amour...* From the American: *it smells like ass in here...* From between my love's cheeks I sing my song of *merde that's good.* Thank goodness for alternatives to "penis" & "anus." Thank goodness for cocks & Rimbaud & butts & sonnets & amour & ass & Verlaine & dicks in the relentless middle of summer in Lubbock.

Oh, Lubbock. Why did I choose you? How did my boyfriend choose to come with me? The name makes me think "buttock" & "banana" & "hammock." So why isn't Lubbock the new Fire Island or P-town? For months I dreamt it was, could be. I was teenage me again—dreaming of making out, moving in with Jake Gyllenhaal, dreaming of the day I could bring a boyfriend, a Jake, home. At times I thought, *If only*, & tried to see myself picking out nightstands with Maggie Gyllenhaal. Now I see even a little gay sex & French poetry would make some folks better citizens. Now there's my Jeff, who fixes the computer, fixes us dinner, fucks my face et mon âme. Isn't that enough of a gay paradise? All we need is another couple for mahjong. Or one other person plus "Lily," what one online mahjong guide calls the imaginary missing player. What an absurd concept. A beautiful name. Lily, come over. Lily, let's watch your favorite movie. Do you prefer comedy, drama, action, or movies with Jake Gyllenhaal in them? Do you like spicy foods? My boyfriend does not but I love him anyway. Lily, whom do you love? & is it possible to hold hands with your love, on the brightest street, in the bustle & heat of your town?

Lily, after another round of mahjong, let's imagine a Lubbock we'd want to live in. Let's ask our favorite imaginary missing players to help. Ask Rimbaud to come, & maybe not date a gun-toting French Symbolist, this time. Ask Verlaine to come, to put down his absinthe, his pistol. Let's say, come back, come to Lubbock, come a big creamy load on all the bullshit. Instead of huddling in the corner of Maxey Park, let's make Lubbock Gay Pride stream through 34th Street, through Buddy Holly Avenue. Let's bring back the best slang term for homosexual—"cockpipe cosmonaut." Let's shout. Let's make sure every homogleam naughtycosm gets good food, good rest, gets the goods of marriage without having to get married. Let's holler, troublemongers. In the lick of many summers.

The School of You

Suppose you live a long life. Full
of blueberries & jade
blazers & dreams of ice skating in the nude

& ice skating in the nude. So briskly
frisky! A life
longer than you planned to live to. You.

Who was told at 13 to die, that you would
soon, a silly
faggot & not even

a white one, just a brief, brief
filth, not worth the spit
to wipe away.

At 13, you knew
you wouldn't last forever. Still, you were given
little reason to believe

you might last another decade,
another. How already you were supposed to be
not. & yes, I am

talking to myself. Saying, suppose
otherwise. Suppose a life so long & gorgeously
silly, viewers will complain

about everything
left out from your biopic,
which will star an actor so handsome

every audience member will gasp,
in unison, upon first seeing him on screen—but
despite that, yes, the fans

will cry: Not enough about that time
he robbed a crêperie!
Not enough about his years spent painting

hippos! Never enough
about how that involved both paintings of
& paintings on hippos, & how long

it took him to realize he was not
very good at painting,
then realizing, finally, that it didn't matter, so long

as his very handsome fingers
spent all those many years dreaming
with paint, & why do only successes get to be

smashing, why not a smashing
failure! Yes, I am
talking to myself

as though it is my birthday. & this is my gift:
telling myself
what I was never told:

suppose in one part of your (still 3-hr-long) biopic
it is your 88th birthday. All day
you exclaim, *I'm 88!* At your party—*I'm 88!*

to every friend & fellow
80-something silly faggot. You are wearing
someone's worst nightmare & you are

who wore it best. & then
the cake? Not 88 candles, but still
a ridiculous number. Flames

& flames. Suppose you blow them out, wishing
for more blazing, more
you. Suppose you

know already: there will be.

Zombie Kindnesses

after Sandra Louise Skoglund

If heterosexuality must continue, let there be cats,
glowy green ones, why not, like alien moss or undead
neon, but definitely cat-shaped & capable of appearing

anywhere—say, a living room in which my grandmother sighs
again, asks again, *Why can't you find a nice girl,*
have some kids? Or, a classroom,

a grad school classroom, where in the middle of a break time
conversation about who we're dating, a straight classmate
puts his hand on my shoulder & earnestly, almost sweetly, wonders,

But with your boyfriend, how do you decide who does what during,
you know?   Let me summon the cats.
Let two of them spook my grandmother

just enough so that she's more concerned with finding an exorcist
than finding me a wife. Let three of them scratch
& scratch my straight classmate's hand. Let them leap

to my rescue, let them henceforth be known as my guardian
screeches, furred veracities, zombie
kindnesses, risen from some unkillable

queer soil. & right now, in the stale mouth
of my dentist's waiting room, I may require all of them,
every green cat. Here,

where not only is every magazine's cover story
about a heterosexual divorce from five years ago,
but also, on one otherwise blemishless wall, hangs a portrait

that must be new, as I
110% would've remembered it, this
framed painting of my dentist &, who else could she be, his wife,

the two of them dressed in sweater vests with little
embroidered badminton racquets
while holding, what else could they be, badminton racquets.

& they're smiling, smiling
like they're the perverts who've just invented dentistry.
Yes.

I need all of you, all your splendidly
obnoxious, scary verdantness.
Firstly because couple's outfits are unacceptable

except on me & my boyfriend. Secondly because I like badminton
but who enjoys badminton that much?
Thirdly because ew.

I beseech you. I have the fanciest of feasts waiting for you.
Rise up. & finally become
such uncompromising visual artists. Come paint

over this beaming monstrosity. Paint instead the glory
of my eye-roll, my whole-body
sigh-snort, my soul

scowl, my profound frown.

Lunar New Year

Never did I imagine you
gifting him a 红包. Never did I imagine
you gifting him a 红包 on 新年,
on our 新年.
Never could I have imagined you,
standing on our doorstep one cold yet bright
February afternoon & saying, 这是给
他的, then handing me
a 红包 for him.
So 红, this 包, so unimaginable
for you, my mother, who never
imagined my life
as a life, not really, not
with him, never with a 他.
Never did I imagine your not, your never,
your always capital N No
unraveling. I'm still having trouble
imagining you
like this. Imagine that: me, beaming, leaping
for this. A rain
droplet of a thing, really.
A real glimpse,
gleam finally,
of flowers.

Spring

Seventy-five degrees & we're three *ready for this!* queers in the most flattering
 shorts.

Three queers ordering too much ramen or just enough, who can say.

Three queers in a FedEx, ready to print poems for a long overdue queer salon.

Three queers drinking definitely too much coffee, three queers & I'm the one
 visiting for just the weekend, so let's stay up talking, talking.

I mean, have I told you yet about going to my omelet place for lunch the other
 day & this guy I overheard?

How I was in the middle of eggy arugula bliss when he said, *Bi-sex-u-al*, all
 slow like that, to another guy, as though it were a new type of omelet,
 though maybe it is, let's ask the waiter?

Did I tell you how he went on, *That's what Sarah told us yesterday*, & the other
 guy clicked his tongue like, *I'm sorry to hear*, & the first guy said,
 Bisexual, quickly this time, quieter, *She must've heard it on TV, from
 her friends, you know, she's only fourteen*?

& then he sighed, *Only fourteen, already deciding to ruin her life*, & then I almost
 said, *What the fuck are you saying*, almost leapt out of my chair to ask the
 other guy, *Why the fuck are you fucking nodding*, but I didn't, I got scared,
 no, not of them, of my hands, how my hands had curled into fists—

Three queers remembering *but you're only fourteen!*

Three queers talking about last week.

Three queers feeling like twenty, drinking ever more coffee, telling sleep to go
 bother the straights.

Three queers staying up until late becomes early.

The School of Eternities

Do you remember the two types of eternity, how we learned
about them in a Wegmans parking lot, when you turned

on the radio, the classical channel? Why
were they even talking about eternity, what

did it have to do with the suddenly
broody guitars? You had a peach

Snapple, I remember the snappy kissy sound of the lid
coming off in your hand. *One type of eternity,* they said, *is inside*

of time, as endless time—life
without death. We were inside our Toyota. I said, *We need*

a new umbrella. Do you remember
when we first rhymed? Do you remember the first time I asked

you about the rain, the expression,
"It's raining cats & dogs," whether it was equally cats & dogs,

falling? Can you remember when you learned the word
"immortality"? The hosts on the classical channel

were okay, I thought you'd do a much better job. I remember saying
so, while you drove us home. Our apartment, our

third. Remember the day we moved
into our first? The boxes of books & boxes of

books? My books? Our sweating up three flights of the greenest
stairs? & you said, *Never again*? & the again, & again,

&? The other type of eternity is outside of time, beyond it,
no beginning, no end. I remember. Your hand, the lid, your hands,

the steering wheel, your lips, your lips. The way you took a sip,
gave me a kiss, before starting

to drive.

Do you remember the first time you drove
me home, before "home" meant where we both lived, the books

on the shelves, the books in the closet
when I ran out of shelves, the second apartment, West

Texas, remember the dust, the flat, another type of eternity, that dusty
sun? & driving

to the supermarket, what was it called
there? & that hand soap we'd get, which scent

was your favorite? I don't remember what it was called, can't
remember exactly the smell,

but your hands, after washing, I remember
kissing them. Don't you remember when we thought

only some things were ephemera?
Can you remember when you learned the word

"ephemera," the word "immortality"? Probably the latter
first, & isn't that something,

immortality first, then menus
& movie tickets. What was the first nickname, the fifth

umbrella, the type of taco you ordered on our sixteenth
trip, remember driving, remember when we thought the world

of the world, remember how I signed the letter
explodingly yours, do you remember you were

driving, we were halfway home, only eight minutes
from Wegmans, remember when we measured distance

in terms of Wegmans, like it was a lighthouse
or pyramid or sacred tree, remember when your name

was Fluttersaurus Vex & mine
wasn't, remember when I lived like a letter, falling

in cartoonish slow-mo down four flights of stairs, did you picture
a letter of the alphabet or a letter I'd written

to you, remember when I asked you about the rain, when
the wizard jumped out, when I lied & you laughed, when I lied

& I lied & I lied, can you remember
last night, how I crossed my arms

as though dead & arranged just so, how I pictured my face
polished, as though alive, &

no, you can't remember
that, since it happened while you were sleeping & I

wasn't, I was up, wondering why people always talk about death
as sleep, & how much I love sleep, hate death,

& have I told you about the student who said, *I'm really,
really afraid of death*, just like that,

in class, it was fitting, because it was poetry
class, ha ha, & I loved it, her saying that, I wanted to say I loved it,

but couldn't, I was thinking about you sleeping
& me not, about me sleeping

& you not, & what even is outside of time, beyond
then, now, no

thanks, I'd prefer the type of eternity where we
are inside, are

us, & last night's movie good,
not great, a stray piece of popcorn still under

our coffee table.

Do you remember when the world
signed the letter *yours ephemerally?*

Remember when I asked you about the rain,
the cats & dogs of it,

if it was 50% cats, 50% dogs, 100%
falling, & you said, *Of course?*

& you said, *She's gotten, the flight's not till, I'm going
to drive.* I remember you

driving to your mother, West Texas
to Upstate New York, you didn't make it in time, she had little time,

then none. I remember your face pressed
into my shoulder. I remember your mother was an endless,

a question your face asked into my shoulder. How I wanted it
to answer because I couldn't. I didn't go

with you, when I could've, I chose a poetry reading
instead, thought, she'll be there, you'll be, is memory the best

eternity we can make?
The only?

& you said it's equal, the cats & dogs raining
down, though in terms of overall

volume. The rain, it's all the different breeds of cat, of dog, & see,
there are more individual cats, since there are more

very large breeds of dog,
the cats have to balance things out

with their number, but the dogs, don't you worry, they're raining
down, too, & they're rain,

absolutely, they're still rain, the cats & dogs,
lots of water for the plants, for the flowers, for the whole street

& our dusty car windows, for the cats & dogs
on the ground, the cats & dogs

that aren't rain, at least
not yet, & maybe that's another

eternity, the rainy type.

I remember you drove us home.
The radio was on. We made a sound like a lid coming off.

Spring Summer Autumn Winter

I pushed my face toward
the sleeping radiator. I smelled a form
of justice. I wanted to be a poet. I waved
my living hands, dead
coupons. I watched him brush
his teeth. His teeth glinted
gorgeous. I stumbled.
Cartwheeled. I said, I will always fight
alongside you in the fight
against tartar buildup. I said, I will.
I said, Thank God without believing
in thanks. I thought what my parents did,
that wasn't poetry. I believed
what white people said about my parents.
I had to say, Stop.
Stop believing them.
I suckled. Pickled. Made mistakes
about octopi. Wore a blue jockstrap
& took pictures. Accepted stickers of astounded
apples from friends. I was a wind
smooching another wind, who had
very good teeth. I was a name
everyone in America thought they were saying
right. Even he thought so.
Then asked, Is that right?
I pushed my face toward the noisy radiator.
Its clang & labor & here.
In bed I touched his voice
in his belly. I touched his Goodnight. He said it always
like it was important.
It was important. I believed in
the Silver Millennium. I said, Sailor Neptune,
one day, a poem for you.

I said, Sailor Neptune, teach me the Deep
Submerge, the Submarine Reflection, the thunderously
turquoise hair. I was a name
in America & would forget I belonged
to my teeth.
I dropped a single wish down the cavernous
mailbox. He would ask,
Is that right? He would bring
a single microwaved donut on a blue napkin at dusk.
He would leave me alone
with my poems. O
if I could lick all your toes at once. I would
write that poem. I loved him,
I told him. I loved him,
so told him about the dream.
The dream starred my parents, stars
of a death metal band's
debut music video. They danced
like everyone was watching. It was important. Their arms
were poems. They said, So what
if we misspell "auditorium," so fucking what—
we'll always say
your name right.
They pushed their faces toward me.
Their poems toward me.
They leapt & thrashed, they were stars,
stars, stars.
I woke up weeping. Do you understand?
I thought I could only fall asleep
doing that.

The School of the Unschoolable

See the stars nightly
    disobeying the night.

Watch the pattering rain
    sketch an anarchist's

map to the future, then
unpattern it away—

        an anarchist's revision.

Praise my mother

who wears a plaid hoodie
    over a polka dot sweater
    over a simply
        brown sweater.

Praise your fashion icon,

though I doubt she's
as iconoclastic.

        Prove my doubt

so wrong.

    Call the sun
the heterophobe
        it's always been.

Never stop babbling
        to old friends or
        fields about your earliest

                whiff of banana bread.

Lick the sad
        from the sea & on
        a Tuesday.

                Flabbergast
        in some earthly

                mouthful of a way
        & tonight.

The School of Joy / Letter to Michelle Lin

in memory of Tanya Jones

Dear Michelle,

summer was
what? The days
so bright yet
small. Small

me, dragging
my blanket, my
blankness room
to room. You wrote

that I write with joy.
When really it's toward,
walking to
the school of

try again.
Today, I'm trying
to write to you.
& through

those last words
with my student,
my peppy *Thanks!*
in reply to her *Hope*

you have a great time
in L.A.!
Remember L.A.?
Spring & every tree

sleepless. That night
we read together
in Chinatown.
That beautiful

old store, the table
in the back you
& your love filled
with snacks. Joy:

sharing poems,
then prawn crackers,
then more poems
from our sparkly new

first books. & it was
my birthday.
So for your final
poem, you made

sure the song was loud,
the plumpest cake pop
in my hand. Then,
the same weekend, this

news. I read it
in the too-small room
of my phone:
Lubbock. Student.

Texas Tech. Car
accident. My student,
killed in an accident.
Her name.

Her face.
My student, her eyes, her laughing, her still showing up
as "withdrawn" on my roster
a month, two months

after. After I stood
before my class
& said, *Tanya was…*
& *Tanya had…*

& I hate how past
that past tense sounds.
Today I'm telling you
about Tanya.

All her questions
about lines,
rhymes, couplets,
compression, tercets,

turns. The loud
hunger in each syllable
of her asking me,
What's writing a poem like

for a real poet?
Today I'm telling you
about Tanya's
real poems. Lyric

extensions of her
school paper columns
on student life, human
worry, & a belief

in wonder.
& last night
I saw her,
reading from her

first book
with formidable
sparkle, in a bookstore
fabulously packed,

I mean everyone,
the staff, the usually
unimpressed intern,
was leaning in for

another Tanya turn.
Today I'm telling you
about losing her.
What I didn't say

because I couldn't think
of a more joyless word
than "withdrawn."
& how I wrote *Thanks*

to the quickly kind,
automatically *Sorry for*.
How I told myself
Just a student

when I trembled,
just stepping
into the classroom
again, two days ago.

Then the way
my hand tried again:
picked up
the best marker,

the purple one.
Started to make
the letters, big ones.
Started to sing

a little. A one-
word song
to fill the board—

Welcome

♦♦♦

Notes

"Winter [Big smelly bowel…]": This poem was written in 2017. It refers to the Doomsday Clock, a project created and maintained by the Bulletin of the Atomic Scientists. This clock is regularly reset to reflect how close humanity is to apocalyptic destruction—how close to "midnight." According to the Bulletin's website, "The Doomsday Clock is a design that warns the public about how close we are to destroying our world with dangerous technologies of our own making. It is a metaphor, a reminder of the perils we must address if we are to survive on the planet." In 2017, the clock read two and a half minutes to midnight. In 2022, 100 seconds to midnight.

"a small book of questions": This sequence is organized around and inspired by the twelve questions of Bhanu Kapil's collection, *The Vertical Interrogation of Strangers* (Kelsey Street Press, 2001).

"One Year Later: A Letter": This poem relies on the following sources—a tribute to Leinonen by his friend Catherine McCarthy, published in *The Washington Post* on June 18, 2016; accounts from friend Brittany Sted of Leinonen and Guerrero in *The New York Times* on June 14, 2016, as well as in *The Orlando Sentinel* on June 15, 2016; an article by Melissa Chan published in *Time Magazine* on June 13, 2016; and articles in *The Orlando Sentinel* marking the one-year anniversary of the shooting, including one by Kate Santich titled "Mom of Pulse victim Drew Leinonen: 'I am my son's voice.'" In response to the attack, a group of Leinonen's friends, including survivor Brandon Wolf and along with Leinonen's mother Christine, created an LGBTQ+ advocacy organization, The Dru Project. You can learn more about their mission and programs at thedruproject.org.

"In the World's Italianest Restaurant": Justin Chin, author of poetry, essays, and fiction, died on December 24th, 2015, from a stroke related to complications with AIDS.

"The School of Eternities": The sign-off phrase "explodingly yours" comes from Brad Kerr.

Acknowledgments

Many thanks to the editors of the following publications, where poems in this book (often as earlier versions) first appeared:

The Account: "The School of More School";

The Adroit Journal: "The School of Keyboards & Our Whole Entire History Up to the Present," "The School of You," "Lunar New Year";

Asian American Writers' Workshop *The Margins*: "Summer [The sunflowers fall...]";

bath magg: "In the World's Italianest Restaurant," "One Year Later: Her Answer";

The Best American Nonrequired Reading 2016: "I am reminded via email to resubmit my preferences for the schedule" (first published in The Academy of American Poets' Poem-a-Day);

The Best American Poetry 2019: "I Invite My Parents to a Dinner Party" (first published in The Academy of American Poets' Poem-a-Day);

The Best American Poetry 2021: "The School of Eternities" (first published in *Ploughshares*);

Bettering American Poetry Vol. 2: "A Favorite Room" (first published in *Wildness*);

Buzzfeed: "Ode to Rereading Rimbaud in Lubbock, Texas";

Cape Cod Poetry Review: "The School of Your Book / Letter to Jennifer S. Cheng," "Winter [You become increasingly...]";

City of Notions: An Anthology of Contemporary Boston Poems: "The School of Fury" (first published in *HEArt*);

CityVerse in Rochester's *City Newspaper*: "Study Abroad";

The Familiar Wild: On Dogs & Poetry: "a small book of questions: chapter vii" (as "a small book of questions: chapter x"), "ode to my beloveds & brevities";

Glass Poetry: "& then a student stands up, says, *Are you serious?*";

Gulf Coast: "Summer [I have a...]";

The Journal: "Doctor's Note," "The School of Red";

Lantern Review: "The School of a Few or a Lot of My Favorite Things";

The Lifted Brow: "The School of Morning & Letters," "Summer [Your emergency contact...]";

The Map of Every Lilac Leaf: Poets Respond to the Smith College Museum of Art: "Zombie
     Kindnesses";
The Massachusetts Review: "Autumn," "Spring";
The McNeese Review: "The School of Australia";
The Normal School: "we'll be gone after these brief messages";
Oxford Poetry: "Origin Story";
Poetry: "Summer [You are the…]," "Winter [Big smelly bowel…]," "The School
     of the Unschoolable";
The Poetry Review: "Spring Summer Autumn Winter";
Political Punch: Contemporary Poems on the Politics of Identity: "Chen   No Middle
     Name   Chen";
Pulse/Pulso: In Remembrance of Orlando: "Things the Grackles Bring" (as "Things
     the Crows Bring");
Pushcart Prize XLIV: "four short essays personifying a future in which white
     supremacy has ended" (first published in *Foglifter*);
Pushcart Prize XLVI: "Every Poem Is My Most Asian Poem" (first published in
     Hobart);
Raleigh Review: "Higher Education";
Sine Theta Magazine: "Items May Have Shifted," "After My White Friend Says
     So Cool Upon Hearing Me Speak Chinese…";
Tin House: "Winter [The grackles flap…]," "The School of Night & Hyphens";
VIBE: "我疼你";
West Branch: "The School of Logic," "The School of Joy / Letter to Michelle
     Lin";
Winter Tangerine: "Elegy While Listening to a Song I Can't Help But Start to
     Move to," "One Year Later: A Letter," "The School of Song, Uno, &
     Dinnertime" (as "The School of Song").

Excerpts from "a small book of questions" were previously published in *bath
magg*, *Hunger Mountain*, *The McNeese Review*, and *Nat. Brut*. "Study Abroad" and
"Origin Story" were reprinted in *No Tender Fences: An Anthology of Immigrant &
First-Generation American Poetry*. "The School of Morning & Letters" and "The
School of Logic" were reprinted in *What Saves Us: Poems of Empathy and Outrage in
the Age of Trump*. "I Invite My Parents to a Dinner Party" was featured on The
Slowdown podcast as well as Poetry Unbound and has been reprinted in several
anthologies.

My thanks and love to my dissertation committee at Texas Tech for reading and thinking through many of these poems: Curtis Bauer, Jill Patterson, and Michael Borshuk. My thanks and love to BOA for all the support, all the beauty: Peter Conners, Genevieve Hartman, Michelle Dashevsky, Aimee Conners, and Sandy Knight. Loving thanks to Vincent Chong for "Moonlight Photosynthesis," the utterly magical queer Asian work of art that graces this book's cover. Loving thanks to Victoria Chang, Ilya Kaminsky, and Tracy K. Smith for your generous words about this book.

My thanks and love to the following people who've offered sustenance and spark along the way:

Albert Abonado, George Abraham, Paige Ackerson-Kiely, Neil Astley, Catherine Bai, Lorcán Black, Elizabeth Bradfield, Jericho Brown, Marci Calabretta Cancio-Bello, Doug Paul Case, Dorothy Chan, Mary Jean Chan, E Yeon Chang, Jennifer Chang, Jennifer S. Cheng, Kazumi Chin, Katie Cortese, Vanessa Crofskey, Cassandra de Alba, Nancy Dinan, Martín Espada, Aerik Francis, Jay Gao, Sarah Gambito, Aracelis Girmay, Juliette Givhan, Jan-Henry Gray, Roy G. Guzmán, Zach Horvitz, Luther Hughes, Brad Kerr, Porochista Khakpour, Swati Khurana, Anna Jekel, Min Jin Lee, Joseph O. Legaspi, Muriel Leung, Michelle Lin, Sally Wen Mao, David Tomas Martinez, Angelina Mazza, Jennifer Militello, Carly Joy Miller, Tomás Q. Morín, Aimee Nezhukumatathil, Sandeep Parmar, Emilia Phillips, Jen Popa, Nina Mingya Powles, Julian Randall, Emma William-Margaret Rebholz (a.k.a. Billy), Hannah Rego, Kate Simonian, Jessica Smith, Monica Sok, stone, Grace Talusan, Allison Titus, Chris Tse, Jennifer Tseng, Sarah Viren, Stephen J. West, Arhm Choi Wild, Jane Wong, Haolun Xu, Yanyi, and Emily Jungmin Yoon.

To Brandeis colleagues and community: my loving thanks. To colleagues and community at New England College, Stonecoast, Antioch, and UMass Boston: my loving thanks. To my students: thank you for nourishing my days and heart. To *Underblong* brilliances: my glittering love and thank you. To Kundiman family: thank you and love, love, love. To my mother and father, to my brothers: a sunflower, an orchid, a daffodil, a lilac. 我很疼你们。

Dear Sam Herschel Wein: a ripe plump plum for the best plum, you—your true saying, your sweet listening. Dear Mag Gabbert: a cascade of raspberries for you, bringer of such freshness and insight. My thank you and my love, dear first readers, collaborators, co-leapers.

Thank you, Jeff Gilbert. For the jokes, the kisses, this feast of a life. Hey. I love you.

About the Author

Chen Chen was born in Xiamen, China and has lived in Western Massachusetts, Upstate New York, and West Texas. He is the author of a previous poetry collection, *When I Grow Up I Want to Be a List of Further Possibilities* (BOA Editions, 2017), which was longlisted for the National Book Award and won the A. Poulin, Jr. Poetry Prize, the Thom Gunn Award, the GLCA New Writers Award, and the Texas League of Writers' Book Award. In 2019, Bloodaxe Books published the UK edition. He is also the author of four chapbooks, most recently *GESUNDHEIT!*, a collaboration with Sam Herschel Wein. Chen's work appears in many publications, including three editions of *The Best American Poetry*. His poems have been translated into French, Greek, Russian, and Spanish. He has received two Pushcart Prizes and fellowships from Kundiman, the National Endowment for the Arts, and United States Artists. He holds an MFA from Syracuse University and a PhD from Texas Tech University. He was the 2018–2022 Jacob Ziskind Poet-in-Residence at Brandeis University. He serves on the poetry faculty for the low-residency MFA programs at New England College and Stonecoast. He edits the Twitter-based journal *the lickety~split* and with a brilliant team he edits *Underblong*. He lives with his partner, Jeff Gilbert, and their pug, Mr. Rupert Giles.

BOA Editions, Ltd.
American Poets Continuum Series

No. 1 *The Fuhrer Bunker: A Cycle of Poems in Progress*
W. D. Snodgrass

No. 2 *She*
M. L. Rosenthal

No. 3 *Living With Distance*
Ralph J. Mills, Jr.

No. 4 *Not Just Any Death*
Michael Waters

No. 5 *That Was Then: New and Selected Poems*
Isabella Gardner

No. 6 *Things That Happen Where There Aren't Any People*
William Stafford

No. 7 *The Bridge of Change: Poems 1974–1980*
John Logan

No. 8 *Signatures*
Joseph Stroud

No. 9 *People Live Here: Selected Poems 1949–1983*
Louis Simpson

No. 10 *Yin*
Carolyn Kizer

No. 11 *Duhamel: Ideas of Order in Little Canada*
Bill Tremblay

No. 12 *Seeing It Was So*
Anthony Piccione

No. 13 *Hyam Plutzik: The Collected Poems*

No. 14 *Good Woman: Poems and a Memoir 1969–1980*
Lucille Clifton

No. 15 *Next: New Poems*
Lucille Clifton

No. 16 *Roxa: Voices of the Culver Family*
William B. Patrick

No. 17 *John Logan: The Collected Poems*

No. 18 *Isabella Gardner: The Collected Poems*

No. 19 *The Sunken Lightship*
Peter Makuck

No. 20 *The City in Which I Love You*
Li-Young Lee

No. 21 *Quilting: Poems 1987–1990*
Lucille Clifton

No. 22 *John Logan: The Collected Fiction*

No. 23 *Shenandoah and Other Verse Plays*
Delmore Schwartz

No. 24 *Nobody Lives on Arthur Godfrey Boulevard*
Gerald Costanzo

No. 25 *The Book of Names: New and Selected Poems*
Barton Sutter

No. 26 *Each in His Season*
W. D. Snodgrass

No. 27 *Wordworks: Poems Selected and New*
Richard Kostelanetz

No. 28 *What We Carry*
Dorianne Laux

Colophon

BOA Editions, Ltd., a not-for-profit publisher of poetry and other literary works, fosters readership and appreciation of contemporary literature. By identifying, cultivating, and publishing both new and established poets and selecting authors of unique literary talent, BOA brings high-quality literature to the public.

Support for this effort comes from the sale of its publications, grant funding, and private donations.

◆◆◆

The publication of this book is made possible, in part, by the special support of the following individuals:

Anonymous (x2)
Blue Flower Arts
Angela Bonazinga & Catherine Lewis
Jennifer Cathy, *in memory of Angelina Guggino*
Chris Dahl, *in memory of Sandy McClatchy*
Bonnie Garner
Carol T. Godsave, *in honor of Jack Langerak*
James Long Hale
Margaret Heminway
Sandi Henschel, *in memory of Anthony Piccione*
Kathleen Holcombe
Nora A. Jones
Jack & Gail Langerak
Paul LeFerriere & Dorrie Parini
LGBT+ Giving Circle
John & Barbara Lovenheim
Richard Margolis & Sherry Phillips
Frances Marx
Joe McElveney
Boo Poulin
Deborah Ronnen
William Waddell & Linda Rubel
Michael Waters & Mihaela Moscaliuc